Serving God Today

Other Books by Martin and Elizabeth Goldsmith

Martin Goldsmith
God On the Move
Islam and Christian Witness
Jesus and His Relationships
Life's Tapestry
What About Other Faiths

Elizabeth Goldsmith
Getting There from Here
God Can Be Trusted
Roots and Wings

Serving God Today

Going Places
by Elizabeth Goldsmith

Kingdom Life
by Martin Goldsmith

Your Guide to Guidance
by Martin and Elizabeth Goldsmith

OM publishing

Serving God Today first published in 2000 by OM Publishing

06 05 04 03 02 01 00   7 6 5 4 3 2 1

OM Publishing is an imprint of Paternoster Publishing,
PO Box 300, Carlisle, Cumbria, CA3 0QS, UK
and PO Box 1047, Waynesboro, GA 30830-2047, USA
www.paternoster-publishing.com

Going Places
Copyright © 1979 Elizabeth Goldsmith
First published in 1979
Reprinted 1981

Kingdom Life
Copyright © 1988 by Martin Goldsmith
First published in 1988

Your Guide to Guidance
Copyright © 1987 and 1991 by Martin and Elizabeth Goldsmith
First published in 1987 as *Finding Your Way*
First published as *Your Guide to Guidance* in 1991

The rights of Martin and Elizabeth Goldsmith to be identified
as the authors of this work has been asserted by them in
accordance with the Copyright, Designs and Patents Act 1998

*All rights reserved. No part of this publication may be reproduced, stored
in a retrieval system, or transmitted in any form or by any means, electronic,
mechanical, photocopying, recording or otherwise, without the prior permission
of the publisher or a licence permitting restricted copying. In the UK such
licences are issued by the Copyright Licensing Agency,
90 Tottenham Court Road, London W1P 9HE.*

British Library Cataloguing in Publication Data

A catalogue record for this book is available from the British Library

ISBN 1-85078-364-0

Unless otherwise stated, Scripture quotations are taken from the Revised
Standard Version, copyright 1946, 1953, 1971, 1973, by the Division of Christian
Education, National Council of the Churches of Christ in the USA and used by
permission; and
The HOLY BIBLE, NEW INTERNATIONAL VERSION.
Copyright © 1973, 1978, 1984, by the International Bible Society.
Used by permission of Hodder & Stoughton Limited.
All rights reserved. 'NIV' is a registered trademark of the
International Bible Society. UK trademark number 1448790

Cover design by Mainstream, Lancaster
Typeset by WestKey Ltd., Falmouth, Cornwall
Printed in Great Britain by
Omnia Books Ltd, Glasgow

Contents

Going Places — 1

Kingdom Life — 81

Your Guide to Guidance — 157

Going Places

Preparing for Christian service

Elizabeth Goldsmith

Contents

Introduction	5
1 On Your Marks!	9
2 Get Set!	43
3 Go!	75

Introduction

Under Starter's Orders

They were a timid group of eleven men picking their way up the mountain in Galilee. The experience of the last few weeks left them all shattered. Jesus, their beloved leader, had been snatched from them and cruelly murdered. Their sense of desolation and fear drove them all into hiding. And when three days later the women came bursting in, declaring that Christ was risen, for a time their stunned minds refused to believe this complete reversal of the situation. Even repeated appearances of the risen Lord himself had not wholly driven all doubt from their reeling thoughts. Matthew tells us that when Jesus appeared to them for the last time 'they worshipped him; but some doubted' (28:17).

Yet to this bewildered group of poorly educated country men Jesus Christ divulged his last and most urgent wish. 'You are to go into all the world and preach the Good News to everyone, everywhere' (Mk. 16:15, Living Bible). Jesus was imparting to them his own burning desire that everyone everywhere would have the opportunity of learning what he had done for them. These eleven men had just come through a traumatic experience; yet Christ himself had come through infinitely more. He had been engulfed in untold suffering and horror: but it would all be wasted if his disciples were unwilling to play their part. Christ's work on earth was now complete in every detail and he knew he was about to ascend to his Father. There was only one thing left: to burn into the hearts of his chosen followers the absolute necessity of sharing the Good News with others. If they hugged it to themselves, how would the world hear about it? They must be made to see how imperative it was that they should make their Lord's finished work known throughout the world.

So it was that Christ explained his further plan. He would not leave his disciples alone and powerless. The Holy Spirit of Mission was to be poured out on them on the day of Pentecost. It was the Spirit who gave them the motivation and the power to witness for Christ. We see the Holy Spirit stepping into the role of commander-in-chief throughout the book of Acts, directing the new Christians and initiating the tremendous work of taking the gospel of Christ to the whole world.

We read this story 2,000 years later, but the message it brings comes as vividly to us as it did on that first Ascension Day. On us too is laid this compelling command of Christ. No feeling of inadequacy or sense of fear will be accepted as an excuse for us to ignore Christ's directive. We dare not plead unsettled political situations or uncongenial surroundings which make us put our own well-being first. The unequivocal word of Christ comes to each and every one who call themselves a Christian, 'Tell everyone, everywhere, what I have done for them.'

1

On Your Marks!

No child of God can claim exemption from the directive to let the whole world know what Jesus has done. The initial call of Christ to his disciples was to 'Follow me', and its immediate result would be 'and I will make you fishers of men' (Mt. 4:19). So often we hear the question, 'How do I know if God is calling me to his service?' But this is based on a false assumption. God has no special élite, no chosen few who are specially 'called'. God's command comes direct to every Christian to spread the Good News. The question should rather be framed, 'Since God has called me to this tremendous task, what particular part does he want me to play?'

It is therefore essential that every Christian ask God for clear guidance as to his or her sphere of service. For many people this will result in no great change of situation or surroundings. The early Christians were told to evangelize Jerusalem first (Acts 1:8) – essentially those immediately around them. They were to speak to their neighbours, gossip Christ in the markets, share their experience with their friends and relatives. This was the immediate out-working of the first step in Christ's plan. So too today, all of us have a responsibility wherever we find ourselves – in our homes, on the factory floor, at the office, in the supermarket. Christ wants us to be his witnesses wherever we are. But this does not excuse us from examining our present situation. We should be asking the Lord, 'Do you want me to stay here, or is there some other sphere of work you have for me?'

If you have never prayed this prayer before, stop reading and spend a few moments in silence asking God to make his plan for your life clear to you. Ask him for a specific sense of call in your present work, or to lead you on to something else which is his better plan for you. Search your heart too as to whether you are really willing to obey God's call, whatever it is.

How do we find out God's will?

The other day I was talking with a Christian mother about her son who was nearing the end of his university course, but had no idea what he would be doing next. 'I think he expects a light to flash from heaven showing him what to do,' she sighed.

God does sometimes guide us in a vivid or sensational way, but more often he gives a gradual conviction over a period of time. As a girl I heard a graphic description of some of the horrors of Hinduism; and back in the quiet of my room I wrote in my diary: 'Mummy told me today about the Juggernaut in India, and the young widows who are burnt alive on their husbands' funeral pyre, and God told me he wanted me to be a missionary.' But as the years slipped by that could easily be passed off as childish emotionalism. It was much more the deepening conviction as time went on which made me certain that this was God's will for me.

I am involved in part-time work at a missionary training college. The vast majority of the hundreds of students who come to us have had no sensational 'call' from God. In fact I know of only two who received guidance through a vision. For most of them guidance has come through a growing conviction over a length of time, deepened by God-given indications.

The sources of their guidance could be grouped under various headings:

Guidance from the Bible

Jesus stated very clearly that 'Man cannot live on bread alone; he lives on every word that God utters' (Mt. 4:4, NEB). The Bible is the spiritual food on which all Christians need to feed daily if they are to remain spiritually healthy and growing. As we read the Bible devotionally and study it systematically God can speak to us through it and reveal his purposes for us and for the whole world.

It was Paul's study of the Old Testament which, under the guidance of the Holy Spirit, revealed to him the eternal purposes of God, deepening his understanding of present salvation and future glory. Hudson Taylor, studying the book of Ezekiel, was gripped by the challenge of chapter 33: 'You, son of man, I have made a watchman . . . you shall give them warning from me. If . . . you do not speak to warn the wicked . . . his blood I will require at your hand' (verses 7ff.). The principle of the awesome responsibility which the servant of God bears lay like a heavy burden on Taylor. Finally he knew he had to found a new missionary society to discharge this God-given task.

In this age of instant foods and automatic machines many are tempted to try to find short-cuts. But there are no instant recipes for finding out God's will. The Bible urges us to 'do your best to present yourself to God as one approved, a workman who has no need to be ashamed, rightly handling the word of truth' (2 Tim. 2:15). Not the random picking at Scripture, but the regular reading of God's Word, reveals his will.

God may speak to us through the whole tenor of Scripture or through some particular passage. I shall never forget the time when my husband and I were working as missionaries in Singapore. We enjoyed our work tremendously, but one day the directors informed us that another couple had been appointed to our position. I was shattered, feeling this could not be the Lord's will. The next morning in *Daily Light* I read: 'The Lord has said to you, you shall never return that way again' (Dt. 17:16). Over the next few days in my Bible reading and through devotional messages the same message was repeated several times. I knew it was the Lord speaking, but it took some months before my bitterness of heart melted. How thankful I was later for that clear word from God which made me willing to unclasp my clinging fingers from a situation which was no longer God's will for us.

Advice from more mature Christians

On his second missionary journey Paul came into contact with a young Christian called Timothy. Immediately we read that Paul wanted Timothy to accompany him. Evidently Paul saw the potential of this recent disciple. There were latent gifts which Paul longed to develop, so he took the initiative and approached the younger man.

In our churches today there is a great need for older Christians to be on the look-out for emerging gifts in the younger generation. Too often responsibility is firmly held in the hands of more mature Christians, providing little opportunity for growth in leadership among others.

Similarly there needs to be an atmosphere of openness between the younger and the older generations. The former needs to be able to come and say, 'I'm too emotionally involved to see myself objectively. Looking at me realistically what gifts do you feel God has given me? Into what kind of situation could you see me fitting? What should I be concentrating on so as to develop my God-given potential to the full?'

Col. 3:15 speaks of being 'called in one body', that is, as part of Christ's body. Our call comes in the context of the fellowship of his people. We see this very vividly in the life of Paul. He had received his commission direct from God at his conversion (Acts 9); but appears to have done little itinerant evangelism for a number of years (Gal. 1:17–2:1). It was only after involvement in the expanding work at Antioch that new impetus came. While Paul was worshipping and fasting with other leaders of the church, God spoke clearly: 'Set aside for me Barnabas and Saul for the work to which I have called them' (Acts 13:2). The stimulus for Paul to set off on his travels came in the context of a united group of Christians worshipping and praying together. So began Paul's fruitful years of missionary activity, travelling through much of the known world, and culminating in his amazing statement 'that from Jerusalem and as far round as Illyricum (Albania) I have fully preached the gospel of Christ' (Rom. 15:19).

We hear much today of the church as the body of Christ. One of the functions of a body is to recognize the abilities given to its various members and actively to encourage and foster them. We say, 'What a waste!' when we see someone with musically-gifted fingers frittering away their time instead of developing their talent. Are we as members of a local church looking out for gifts in others? Do we believe in God the Holy Spirit sufficiently to realize that even the quietest member of our church has some gift from God (Eph. 4:7)? Are we attempting in every way possible to lead each member to develop their gifts to the full?

If you already have a sense of call into some form of service for God tell someone else about it. Keeping a feeling like this to yourself will often result merely in abstract emotional vagueness. If God has really called you then your call can stand up to the close scrutiny of a friend. Discuss your feelings with an older Christian whose advice you respect. The fact of verbalizing the situation will help you to see it more objectively. The maturity and experience of the other person may well reveal flaws which were hidden to you. On the other hand if after prayerful consideration they whole-heartedly support your action this will be confirmation to you of God's guidance.

A few months ago I was talking with a girl from Scotland who was quite prepared to go overseas as a missionary if only she was sure God had called her. As we discussed together her very good training, excellent health, stable background and prayerful concern for missionary work over a number of years it became apparent to us both that the Lord was not going to give her a spectacular 'call'. He had quietly removed all obstructions and placed in her heart a real desire for missionary work. She need not wait any longer. This *was* God's call to her.

On the other hand, another girl who was very much drawn to work among Spanish-speaking people came to see, through discussion with older friends, a deep sense of inadequacy in her own life. Eventually she realized that it would be most unwise to go overseas until her own problems had been overcome. In many ways she was an outgoing, capable girl, and it was only through careful advice that these areas were revealed.

The Bible knows nothing of isolated Christians. If you do not have a church behind you to which you can turn for advice and guidance, you need to ask God to help you find one. The isolated joints of the body cannot live on their own, and no more can we. If God has placed you in a church where you have little spiritual fellowship and yet you feel God has set you there for a purpose, ask him to give you one or two praying friends with whom you can discuss Christian things at the deepest level. God delights to answer prayers like this! If he is to call you into the ministry in this country or to overseas work, you will need these friends to stand behind you. And for the present too their advice and support will be invaluable.

Missionary society leaders will gladly make themselves available to discuss the future of any who are seriously considering overseas work. Their experience has made them well able to evaluate candidates potential usefulness and how easily they would fit into work overseas, and they are available without obligation. If you are feeling the need for advice write to a leading missionary society, or take yourself to one of their conferences. Here you will have more leisure to learn in depth from experienced workers about opportunities in other countries, and to discuss your own future plans.

Those who feel God is calling them to a 'full-time' ministry in this country should seek out a godly minister for prayerful consultation. He or she will be able to explain the usual steps leading to ordination. It should however be realized that although most missionary societies and some major denominations practise careful screening of their potential candidates, other denominations do not. It is therefore doubly important that those who seek ordination should submit their call to close scrutiny. Much heartache can be experienced when, through an initial youthful emotionalism, people find themselves with responsibility which God has not fitted them to bear.

In emphasizing the fact that God often guides through the body of the church we must not limit God by disallowing specific individual guidance. There may be times when advice from other Christians, however well-meaning, is totally misplaced. Paul had to contend with this on his last trip to Jerusalem. Being vividly warned of the threatened dangers which lay ahead of him, his close friends begged him not to go on. In situations like this great humility and God-given wisdom are needed to be sure that sticking to one's original plan is not mere pig-headedness!

Mission candidate committees and ordination selection boards have been known to be proved wrong. Gladys Aylward was turned down as quite unsuitable for missionary work and incapable of learning a foreign language! Yet the advice of experienced leaders has proved a great help to many younger Christians.

Circumstances

Our heavenly Father is not only the God who redeemed us by his love, he is the God who created us and moment by moment sustains this world we live in, as many of the Psalms reveal. Our circumstances are entirely ordered by the Lord.

The story of Jonah describes with unusual clarity how God can and does use the forces of nature to display his will. The fearful storm sent by God exposed Jonah's sin and made him willing to confess his disobedience in attempting to flee from God. The great fish which appeared so miraculously preserved Jonah's life. Then came the lessons taught through nature, first by the luxuriant growth of a tropical plant and then by the activities of a tiny worm.

It takes the eye of faith to see that our circumstances are the direct ordering of our sovereign heavenly Father; yet this is one of the most frequent ways the Lord uses to show us his will. As we approach a decision point in life we can pray that God will close all other doors except the one he wants us to go through. I remember the keen disappointment I felt at being turned down when I made my first application for a teaching post – until a friend pointed out that, as I had prayed about it, I should instead be thanking the Lord that he had given such a clear answer!

Paul arrived in Rome in circumstances far different from what he could have wished. He found himself a prisoner, restricted to his own house (Acts 28:16). But he joyfully accepted the limitations that God had put on him, and set about doing what he could. Not long after, he could write, 'The gospel . . . has become known throughout the whole praetorian guard' (*i.e.* Caesar's personal body-guard; Phil. 1:13). God used the circumstances of Paul's imprisonment to bring the message into an area which might otherwise have been extremely difficult to reach.

Circumstances are at times used by God to close the door to a particular opportunity and at other times to open it.

A highly qualified nurse was completing her missionary training not long ago. For many years she had had a deep sense of call to work in a particular Asian country, and staff and students alike felt how suitable she would be for this type of work. Then it was discovered she had an incurable back disease which completely excluded the possibility of life in a tropical climate. She fought an agonizing battle. How could she give up her long-standing desire? Had not God himself put this great love in her heart?

But God's guidance through this circumstance could not be evaded. Peace in acceptance has now led on to a fruitful and unusually influential ministry in nursing training in her own country.

Another woman who longed to serve God overseas was kept in this country by her responsibility to her elderly mother. She found great fulfilment and much joy in lecturing in a Bible College which trained others for overseas work. Then within a few months the Lord took her mother and the Bible College closed down, freeing her completely to become a missionary herself. God's hand overruling her circumstances was so unmistakable she knew clearly the time had now come to go overseas herself.

Deep inner peace

When someone is seeking the Lord's guidance for their lives the above three strands often dovetail together leading to a deepening conviction as to God's will. If the Lord has guided you through the directing of his word, if this has then been confirmed through advice from older Christians, and if God has ordered your circumstances so as to set you free to move forward – now is the time to act.

God has promised to guide us; many times in Scripture he has told us so. (See Pss. 32:8; 48:14; Is. 58:11; Jn. 16:13.) Our heavenly Father longs far more than we do that we should know his will and do it. We can have every confidence in him. And he has pledged himself that if we begin to step out of his path he will tell us clearly: 'Your ears shall hear a word behind you, saying, "This is the way, walk in it," *when you turn to the right or when you turn to the left*' (Is. 30:21), that is, when and if we turn *out* of God's path he will speak to us. Therefore if we are not aware of his saying anything to us, and we are honestly desiring to do his will, we can quietly rest in the assurance that our present attitudes are what he wants.

With a small child the parent has to be constantly guiding: 'Don't do that! You might get hurt! Don't go there; that's someone else's garden!' As the child grows older, the necessity for constant verbal correction is past. The parental directives need be far less frequent. So it is with our heavenly Father. If he sees us walking in his will he has no need to speak to us about it. It is only when we are about to do something which displeases him that he must make us aware of it.

Col. 3:15 says, 'Let the peace of God rule in your hearts.' The word 'rule' could also be translated 'arbitrate' (as between two opposing parties) or 'act as umpire'. The latter brings to us a very vivid picture: so long as the ball remains on the field and the players refrain from fouling the game can proceed. It is only when something goes wrong that the umpire sounds his whistle. In the same way, as long as the peace of God reigns in our hearts we can be sure that we are in God's will. If we find ourselves feeling restless or anxious about something we need to pray specifically that God will show us what the trouble is.

God sometimes sends a holy restlessness; as with the person who said to me, 'I enjoy my work. I have a super church and there's so much to do for God here – but sometimes I feel so unsettled inside.' This young man came to see that although God was using him greatly where he was, he now wanted him to move on.

Remember, God's work needs our very *best* young people, not those who are sitting on the side-line. Paul and Barnabas were two of the most gifted leaders in Antioch, but the Lord decreed that they were to be the ones to go. If your talents are being greatly used right where you are, that is no reason to suppose that God might not want to move you on. Today is the training school for tomorrow. God may have an even richer ministry for you.

Other points on guidance

Wherever we look in the world today there is desperate need on all sides. Those who are unwilling merely to shrug their shoulders but want honestly to face up to current situations face a tremendous dilemma. Where does one begin? The more one looks, the more one becomes aware of untold suffering and spiritual deprivation. So the question arises: 'Does the need constitute the call?' Does the sheer fact of physical want and spiritual poverty automatically mean that we should do something about it?

As we read the Gospels, we notice that Matthew's 'Go and preach' is paralleled by John in 20:21: 'As the Father has sent me, even so I send you.' When we consider in what spirit he was sent – a spirit of constant service and ministry to every level of human need – we realize how wide our commission is. Nevertheless even our Lord faced the sheer physical impossibility of coping with every demand made on him. He had prayerfully to discern his Father's will and concentrate on the work to which his Father had sent him. Several times we read that he withdrew, consciously turning his back on the need, so as to save his strength for priorities. So we too dare not respond to every need around us, but only to those about which God himself gives us a special concern.

The answer to the above question may lie in the fact that the need does not necessarily constitute the call; but a deepening awareness of one particular need over a length of time may be God's way of speaking to us.

A friend of ours, with high qualifications on the technical side, is privileged to come from a church where there is excellent Bible teaching. During the last two years the churches in one part of Africa have been repeatedly drawn to his attention. Although evangelistic outreach through these churches is good, there is a great lack of clear teaching on the

Christian life. The need for consistent Bible exegesis applied in a practical way to everyday life has impressed itself upon him. As he prayed about it, he now feels increasingly that this is God's call to him to fill that gap. He has come to the place where he is willing to lay aside his technical skills because of the consistent pressure from the Lord that there are other more important things in life.

Your own unique background and training may have specifically fitted you for a particular work. Jesus prepared his disciples so well that when the time came to evangelize the formerly much-hated Samaritans the barriers were already down. In Acts 8 the disciples went straight into this completely new work without any inward trauma or conflict. Your family background or previous experience may well be fitting you for a work which someone else would find extremely difficult. Ask God to highlight for you what lessons he has been teaching you and what gifts he has given.

Don't be surprised if feelings of inadequacy surge up inside you at times. Many have felt the same before you. Jeremiah expostulated: 'I do not know how to speak, for I am only a youth' (Je. 1:6). Centuries before that, Moses used the same excuse, 'I am not eloquent . . . but am slow of speech'. Again and again God assured him that he would be with him, and this was all that mattered. We think today of Moses and Jeremiah as being among the great prophets of old, and sometimes forget that they started out with much trepidation. It was only as they took the risk of obeying that they grew into greatness.

As your interest in a certain type of work grows, set yourself to find out more about it. Added information can confirm or contradict a sense of call. From a distance some types of home ministry and some overseas situations may appear very romantic. But face to face with the concrete reality it will be seen in quite a different light. Our Lord had very strong words to say about those who failed to count the cost (Lk. 14:28). It is no use going into a situation with blinkers on. The more information you can discover, the more easily God can set the course for your life.

It is essential that everyone considering the possibility of 'full-time' service for Christ should face up to the sacrifices involved. Ministers of religion in Britain are amongst today's lowest-paid workers. They do not always experience the respect given to their status in previous decades. In fact 'turning your collar round' may bring a painful isolation from the general public. Full-time evangelists are forced to be away from home and family for many weeks in the year. The travelling secretaries for organizations like the UCCF often suffer from a great sense of rootlessness as they rarely come back to their home base.

In a foreign country the tensions may be even greater. Much has already been written about culture shock with its attendant difficulties, and this is not the place to go into these aspects fully. But intending graduates should face squarely the threat to their own identity which comes through being made to feel like children again because of inadequate language and no knowledge of how to behave in even the simplest relationships. And when you feel you are beginning to master the foreign language, the difficulty of using it actually to win someone for Christ may appear insurmountable, especially in a country which has been steeped in other religions for centuries. Women need to pray through on their knees the cost of remaining single, since a large proportion of those going overseas will never marry. The marrieds face heart-rending tension due to long periods of separation from their children. Missionary wives have been said to be among the most lonely people in the world because of the work-demands made on their husbands. All must think through the cost to their own elderly parents who will now have to manage without the son or daughter for whom they have sacrificed so much in earlier life.

Nevertheless, if you are aware that God is speaking to you, there is only one proper response, and that is obedience. Your heavenly Father knows all the repercussions your obedience will bring. He has already prepared for them. The consequences are his.

You cannot guide a stationary car. You must switch on the engine, engage the gear and move forward. God has pledged himself to guide you as you move forward in response to his command. Write to a missionary society or training college, speak to the minister of your church, or take whatever action you feel God is leading you into. And be confident in his promise, 'The Lord your God is with you wherever you go' (Jos. 1:9).

Our aim

The prophet Habakkuk, baffled by the violence and godlessness around him, glimpsed a truth which steadied his wavering faith. 'The earth will be filled with the knowledge of the glory of the Lord, as the waters cover the sea' (2:14). We too, who have seen the glory of God revealed in Jesus Christ, long for the day when every group in society and every race throughout the world should come face to face with this glory.

Paul was gripped by his commission 'to make all people see what is the plan of the mystery hidden for ages in God who created all things' (Eph. 3:9). Whatever our particular calling, we too 'have been destined and appointed to live for the praise of his glory' (Eph. 1:12).

The special task of mission was outlined step by step by our Lord in the Great Commission (Mt. 28:16–20).

'Go therefore and make disciples of all nations,' he commanded. Evangelism of the whole world was the goal he had in mind. Each new generation requires to be shown what Christ has done for them. As outlooks and culture change, the gospel needs to be presented in relevant terms to the rising generation. Methods which were suitable twenty years ago must be re-appraised, and the emphasis made to correspond with the felt needs of the listeners, from whatever background they come.

Evangelism is usually most effective when undertaken by someone of the same race and cultural background as the listener. This helps to eliminate any feeling that Christianity is a foreign religion. For this reason foreigners in this country, or nationals overseas, are often best reached by their own people. However, in churches which are weak or lacking in vision, outsiders may still serve as catalysts to stimulate outreach. And certain areas remain where there are no churches at all. Churches in the homelands could often benefit from a renewed emphasis on reaching out beyond the narrow confines of their own community. The recent visits of Christian leaders from South America and Africa have prodded some European churches into re-thinking their own evangelistic programme.

'Baptising them in the name of the Father and of the Son and of the Holy Spirit.' This clearly speaks of planting churches. Men and women are not only to be called to follow Christ, they are to confess him openly in baptism, and to come together to form churches. This is an integral part of the task of mission, whether we are working on a new housing estate in this country, an industrial area of a huge Japanese city, or a tribal village in a remote part of New Guinea. It was never our Lord's intention that new Christians should remain isolated.

In order that these new churches will be built up and strengthened, our Lord continued: 'Teaching them to observe all that I have commanded you.' This covers the whole area of Bible teaching and continuous training of all members, from the newest convert up. Here is a vast area of opportunity for service for all Christians. Some will be able to give their leisure hours to running a youth club or teaching Sunday School. Others by extending hospitality and friendship will encourage the lonely or depressed. Those with gifts of administration will aid the smooth running of the church. Teachers, pastors, helps of all kinds will be needed.

The upbuilding of the church requires loving concern for the physical and emotional needs of the whole person. This will involve the world-wide church in calamity prevention and relief, agricultural projects, medical aid, educational development and all that goes to meet mankind's great variety of needs, following the pattern of our Lord's own ministry.

It must not be forgotten that 'teaching them to observe all that I have commanded you' compels the Christian worker to teach the Great Commission itself to the new converts, who in their turn will teach others also. In nature one feature of living organisms is self-propagation. The Holy Spirit was given to impart life. If there is no form of reproduction there is no true life. A cycle of endless propagation was envisaged by Christ – until we reach our goal: 'This gospel of the kingdom will be preached throughout the whole world, as a testimony to all nations, and then the end will come' (Mt. 24:14).

Home or overseas?

When someone senses the call of God to full-time service, one of the first questions which arises is, 'Does God want me to go overseas or stay in this country?' Although this highlights a natural dichotomy in many people's minds, the difference is not as great as some may think. De-Christianized pagan materialism has become a feature of the western world. Our own homeland is as much in need of missionaries as anywhere else. Indeed the child brought up here today may know little about their Christian heritage and assume that the Bible is a mere collection of folk-tales and myths.

The multi-racial character of many of our large cities brings its problems. A friend of my husband, on being appointed curate in Spitalfields, East London, some years ago, settled down to learn Yiddish. He had discovered that three-quarters of his parish were Jews. Today, following a rapid population change, Christian workers in that part of London would do better to study Bengali.

We were visiting a part of Bradford not long ago and noticed several Sufi restaurants and shop signs. On talking with the local minister it was disquieting to learn that no-one in his church knew anything about this branch of Islam. Here was a 'mission field' less than a hundred yards away with a crying need for someone to understand these Muslim mystics and think through how best they could be won for Christ.

The need for full-time Christian workers in this country cannot be over-estimated. Many of our churches are short of ministers. Country parishes are being forced to link together with one person in charge of four or five villages. Youth specialists are urgently needed for work among schools and colleges. In schools, the abysmal shortage of religious instruction teachers who are genuinely committed to the Christian faith results in the present attitude of the vast majority of our young people towards religion. Among the socially maladjusted, whether actively dropping out or not, there is great need for the Christian message.

If this is true for our own country, how much more do we see an infinite variety of opportunities for serving God overseas. In every walk of life there is need for Christian witness. Within the churches the openings are strategic – for evangelism, Bible teaching, lay training, pastoral care, and the training of ordinands. Mass media provide some of the most effective ways of reaching people's hearts and minds – through radio, television and literature of all kinds. Many professional skills are acutely needed by third-world countries and can be combined with a Christian testimony.

The pressing needs and opportunities clamour for attention on all sides. Each one of us must come humbly to the Master Designer and say, 'I know you have your over-all plan for the world, and you have a work and place for which you are fitting me. Please show me where it is. I am willing to go anywhere for your sake – to stay at home or go overseas, to work with any type of people, with any background. Please make your will clear to me.'

Professional or full-time

My brother was one of the Cambridge Seventy who, back in the late fifties, committed themselves to go anywhere for God. Many of those seventy have travelled to all parts of the world as missionaries; but my brother remained in his profession. He was willing to give it up; yet each time he sought the Lord's guidance he had no peace about moving out. Today God is giving him strategic opportunities for witness in his capacity as an electronics engineer, and bringing people into his life whom few 'full-time' workers would meet. Obviously God cannot want all his servants to be 'full-timers'. The majority are to remain in their jobs and professions and serve God with the added advantage of natural relationships with their surrounding society. The challenge remains for these to keep the original aim of the glory of God as bright as it is for those who are 'specialists'.

Overseas the political situation may necessitate continuing to use one's professional skills. Some countries regard adversely the word 'missionary' on a passport, yet would be only too pleased to use the expertise of an agricultural specialist or construction engineer. An amazing revolution is taking place today in some of the Arab oil states. Areas where no follower of Christ has been allowed to live for centuries now house pockets of Christians from Pakistan, Korea or the West, brought in to help cope with the oil rush. Although proselytizing is forbidden in these parts, the impact of their lives has not gone unnoticed among people who have never even met a Christian before.

Most third-world countries are desperately short of professional skills of all kinds. We who own so much in the West must honestly face up to the challenge of two-thirds of the world who have so little. The Principal of the college where my husband lectures had a striking poster above his desk. It showed a herd of Friesian cows, sleek and contented, quietly grazing in a meadow thick with grass. Then in the bottom corner lies a smaller inset displaying parched hard ground with scattered tufts of vegetation on which a few lean cattle with their ribs almost sticking through their skin attempt to feed. The words across the two pictures state: 'To whom much is given, of him will much be required' (Lk. 12:48).

We have the example of our Lord who cared not only for people's eternal salvation but also for their immediate physical needs. Nearly every skill which is taught in our universities and colleges of further education is urgently required by the under-developed countries. Many of these already obtain help from the secular agencies and have never associated Christianity with this type of aid. A large conference for Chinese Christians in Singapore some years ago was horrified to hear an African brother say, 'In my country I have met many Chinese who have come to bring us technical skills. They were all Communists. I had no idea there were any Christian Chinese!'

Yet there are inevitable tensions when working overseas in a professional capacity. The spiritual needs loom so large that one can regret the hours spent in one's professional capacity, and long to have more time for a purely spiritual ministry. Often expatriates are forced to move in social circles and at a standard of living which cut them off from the large majority of the local people. This inevitably results in local Christians hesitating to be on intimate terms with them. Little or no time is allowed by their company for language study or understanding of the national culture, so the Christianity they bring will unconsciously have many western overtones. They will probably also find themselves on a short-term appointment, as most national companies employ expatriates only until their own people are trained. Developing nations are understandably anxious to reduce their own unemployment.

Despite this, if the draw-backs are faced realistically, and the opportunities grasped imaginatively, a strategic work for the kingdom of God can emerge.

In some circles it is assumed that the day of the 'full-time' missionary is past. This however is far from the truth. Many third-world countries place little or no restrictions on missionary work. National churches are crying out for the help of experienced workers. Bible colleges and theological seminaries overseas are in urgent need of spiritually minded lecturers with good theological training. Repeated requests come for youth workers, both for church fellowships and in places of education. Lay training is a top priority in growing churches with a shortage of ordained ministers. The demand is for those who can train others, whether Sunday School teachers, leaders of women's work, Bible study groups or evangelistic teams.

Missionaries of today are seldom like the young pioneers of former generations going overseas in their early twenties with little or no specialist training. Churches are already established in most countries of the world, with their own gifted leaders. But the national churches still look to the West for the help of mature men and women of God, who have well-developed gifts and can hold their own among national leaders. Many of the third-world churches know much of the vitality and enthusiasm of the Holy Spirit, and they require the older churches to provide the balance of deeper maturity and Bible knowledge.

Working alongside national leaders has tremendous advantages. While contributing their own particular gifts, the missionaries will look to the nationals for advice on language, culture and local customs. The unconsciously 'Western' image of Christianity in so many countries now has a chance of being adapted to become more truly indigenous. Paul and Barnabas were part of an international team working at Antioch, which included also a man from Cyrene (Lucius), a black African (Symeon) and a Jewish court official (Manaen). Each contributed his own particular gifts; and we find the church at Antioch developing a strong individuality under the guidance of the Holy Spirit.

Short-term or long-term?

An increasing number of dedicated Christian young people spend a year or two in short-term service for their Lord. In this country those who are aware of the pressing problems of inner-city situations will find rich cross-cultural experience in assisting such Anglican projects as the Mayflower Centre, Shrewsbury House and the Cambridge University Mission. The various city missions and medical missions do a valuable work. And other projects like the Newham Community Renewal exist to work through church and community activities towards a spiritually and socially renewed society. Groups like Operation Mobilisation and Youth with a Mission also provide good training and many opportunities for an effective witness often in most unusual places. The benefit to the young Christian of a time spent like this is very apparent. Here they learn to mix with all types of people, meeting them on their own wavelength, and chatting naturally about their Saviour.

Skilled short-term workers are valuable in many situations. Tearfund and a variety of missions channel these to positions where their professional abilities can make a great difference. They may be used to dig wells, build dams, set up a small livestock project or train for various types of home craftsmanship. Where a long-term worker is due for a break, a short-termer may often be able to step in with their own particular skill, *e.g.* surgery, occupational therapy, accountancy and teaching. Together with a secular contribution there may well be opportunities for personal evangelism and encouraging local Christians.

Countries where English is the language of education make it much easier for temporary workers to fit in. Or they may find a useful position as a teacher of English. If they are able to communicate freely, at least with the educated people, they may well find opportunities for a spiritual ministry too.

Where some tragedy has struck, such as drought, floods or earthquake, short-term workers are often urgently needed to help with the immediate problem. Even leaving it for a week or two may well be too late. Christians should be in the forefront, providing assistance, where any form of human tragedy cries out for help.

Yet short-term work overseas has its obvious drawbacks. Temporary expatriates cannot hope to have any deep understanding of the local people and their reactions, unless they are fortunate enough to have the loving advice of more permanent workers. Misunderstandings easily arise due to differences of priorities of emphasis between the national and expatriate. It is very difficult to make real relationships when two people do not understand each other's heart language. Unless the newcomers are aware of other people's feelings, they will easily find themselves setting up a western style project, or unconsciously ride rough-shod over national sensitivities.

Much frustration is often experienced by short-term workers who, at best, will have been given a crash course on the local language and culture, and at worst will find themselves thrown in at the deep end.

Yet an experienced mission leader remarked to me the other day, 'The advantage of short-term workers is that they are vividly aware of the need to train others. They know they only have a limited time for the job, so preparing someone else to take their place is their top priority.'

Undoubtedly it involves a greater sacrifice to commit oneself to long-term service overseas. Many considerations have to be taken into account, not least the requirements of one's own children and elderly parents. However, many factors point to a longer period of service being more desirable in the majority of situations.

When envisaging a more permanent commitment it should be possible to set aside adequate time to obtain a thorough grasp of the language. Time should not be felt to be wasted that is spent just living with the local people, getting to know them, appreciating their hopes and fears, and growing acquainted with their own wealth of culture and folklore. After this period of orientation the new recruit's main work can begin, whether Bible college lecturing, church work, assisting medically or in some other way.

We ourselves were painfully reminded of the importance of this period of orientation during our time in Sumatra. A warm-hearted missionary friend of ours, with a doctorate in theology, went straight into seminary teaching with little opportunity to learn the local culture. One Christmas a country church invited him to show slides at their large evangelistic gathering. But his slides showed the life of Christ as depicted in western stained-glass windows. The flat figures in symbolic poses, crisscrossed by black lines, conveyed nothing to them. This complete failure to adjust culturally resulted in total non-communication.

Today it is keenly realized that, as we carry the life-giving message of Jesus Christ it must not be linked with cultural imperialism. It is not our western way of life or outlook which we attempt to impart, but the supra-national message of Jesus Christ. Yet if we come as expatriates for only a limited time our influence is bound to be western.

It is coloured by attitudes of which we are completely unaware, and only prolonged and intimate communication with those from other backgrounds will begin to reveal them to us.

In this country this applies equally to middle-class clergymen in largely working-class parishes, or to middle-aged ministers seeking to relate to a rapidly changing society. Great flexibility and genuine love are needed to motivate them into learning the very different language of the people they serve and their own special culture. Too often the church has attempted to transplant middle-class or out-moded approaches, resulting in strangulation of any newly emerging life.

It is essential that those working in immigrant areas should be aware of the same problem. Here there is no short-term easy answer, but a need for men and women dedicated to giving years of their life to love and appreciate their foreign neighbours. Only in this way will links be formed which can draw them to Christ and build them into a church spontaneously expressing the Spirit's life in their own particular way.

Time is needed for a real friendship to blossom into flower; and only the long-term worker has sufficient of this essential ingredient. Neither an inner-city factory worker, nor a national Christian in a South American village, can be expected to relate deeply with a stranger who comes only for a year or two. Relationships grow slowly. People want to know if we have come as a nine-day wonder, or if we want really to love them and stand alongside them over the years.

Long-term workers also have time to appraise the impact of their work. As they become immersed in the local thought-forms and concepts they may develop the ability to think through methods of evangelism appropriate to the situation. They can help to frame a church order and forms of worship suitable to the environment. And they can reach a new understanding of Scripture, enriched by the local context.

The majority of short-term workers are young. But maturity is a factor which earns deep respect in many third-world countries. Many missionaries thank God for their grey hair! With long-term service the nationals have the opportunity of watching their workers change and mature as people. They will live together and know them intimately at different stages of their lives, watching them bring up their children and increase in spiritual stature. It will be seen that the workers are not just enthusiasts, coming briefly for the novelty of the situation or selfishly to gain some unusual experience. They have come following the example of their Lord, to identify with those around them and to serve them.

Those who return home

Will I stay the course? Is it a disgrace if I have to return home after a few years? Would it be better not to go at all? For a variety of reasons, a number of workers who have committed themselves to long-term service overseas may find themselves back home again. Poor health is often responsible for this situation, or the demands of children's education, or the increasing frailty of elderly parents. Personality clashes are not infrequent, and differences in temperament easily cause growing tension. There are times when the going has been rough and other times when God himself seems to move us on.

For whatever the reason the servant of God has returned home it will still be accompanied by agonizing heart-searching. One cannot lightly go back on what one believed to be the call of God. Necessity demands the deepest baring of the soul to the searching gaze of his Holy Spirit, lest the new situation should in any way have been brought about through selfishness or through missing the will of God.

But we are still the servants of the living God, whether at home or abroad. The Master Potter, with his sureness of touch, has an amazing way of bringing together the shattered pieces of our life. He is not content merely to patch it up: he reworks our lives into a new vessel (Je. 18:1–5), into something which is richer and more Christ-like than ever it could have been without this traumatic experience. There is no failure in coming home. The failure comes when we allow ourselves to listen to the whispered discouragement of the devil that God no longer has a job for us to do.

Many who now serve God in their own country have had their lives and ministry enriched through some time overseas. The experience they gathered has been to their lasting gain. Lessons learned overseas prove most appropriate for this country. Fresh ideas gained are able to enhance the home situation. And the lasting interest in the foreign country where they have served can be shared with others until they too catch the vision.

Qualifications and their use

'I have a degree in geography. How can my training be used in missionary service?'

This type of question is quite justifiable, but omits one important fact. Your heavenly Father may have allowed you the privilege of a higher education, but this does not necessarily mean it is your particular training which he wants to use. God may be looking for something greater: for a trained mind which knows how to think, analyse, assess and make decisions. This will be of vital importance when planning the strategy of evangelizing a certain area or how best to mobilize the laity in a minister-orientated church. Much shoddy and ineffective Christian work here and overseas has resulted from careless planning or lack of trained insight.

Training as a teacher may not necessarily imply that God wishes you to teach your own subject. Rather you may perhaps use your skills to teach spiritual truths and biblical doctrine with clarity and imagination. All mission-work today, in the home ministry and abroad, needs the ability to communicate in the teaching and training of others.

Of course God may wish to use your specific training, and your particular skills may fit exactly into his pattern for your life. And there are many unexpected ways in which previous training may be found useful. I can think of a mission leader with a lawyer's training who has often thanked God for the discipline of mind and reasoning ability which it developed in him. My husband trained as a Russian interpreter, but since university has hardly spoken a word of that language. But as a result of skills learnt he later found that he could move with comparative ease between the closely related Malay languages. Russian Political Thought, which he studied, has been invaluable in his present work on Marxism. German, which was his second language, lay dormant for twenty years, but is now being used in his increasing continental ministry. God has many unexpected surprises and you never know how he will weave your training into the pattern of your future usefulness.

Some people may feel it a real sacrifice to give up the work and training they love so well. Friends and relations may call it a tragic waste. But God has an amazing way of never wasting anything. He knows how to blend all the strands of our life and preparation together. All he wants from us is the willingness to go wherever he wants, to be absolutely at his disposal.

2

Get Set!

Spiritual preparation

As a child I remember gazing at a map of the Sinai Peninsula and wondering why God made Moses take such a circuitous route to the promised land. It was ten years or more before I came across a verse which suddenly made my eyes light up.

'When Pharaoh let the people go, God did not lead them by way of the land of the Philistines, although that was near; for God said, "Lest the people repent when they see war, and return to Egypt" ' (Ex. 13:17). So that was the reason why: the Israelites were not ready for it yet. Later on they would have to go into battle, even to face the mighty Philistine warriors; but not yet.

Any form of service for God will immediately make us a target for the enemy. Ephesians 6:12 gives us a glimpse of his strength. Before moving forward, a time of preparation is essential, and the most important aspect of this is spiritual preparation. We need to spend time with God, getting to know him, studying his word and communicating with him.

We all spend time with our family and friends. Ask yourself how much time you spend alone with God, worshipping him and listening to his voice? Relationships all take time, and this most important relationship of all is worthy of all the time we can give.

Many Christians plan for some part of each day which they specifically reserve for their Lord. It is often first thing in the morning, before the rest of the household begin to move, when we can be sure of being undisturbed. Others find that last thing at night suits them better with the rush of the day behind them. When my children were small, and short broken nights became the usual, I made time in the middle of the morning when the baby went to sleep. The time chosen can suit the individual, but each of us needs to plan a definite time for waiting on God.

Here there will be opportunity to grow in the capacity for worship as we take time to meditate on the greatness of our glorious King. There will be the heart-warming times as we open his word and read his personal message to us, learning to apply its deep truths to the warp and woof of our everyday life. Intercession for others will naturally spring out of a deepening concern for a lost world for whom Christ sacrificed all. And praise and thanksgiving will bubble up out of our growing awareness of God's amazing love and wonderful care for the whole of his creation.

One of the problems of living in a material world is that spiritual things easily become crowded out. With the increasing responsibilities which age and maturity bring the pressure of time becomes even

Get Set!

greater. It is of vital importance that during our early days as a Christian we set the priority of a time alone with God each day.

My husband and I, when in Indonesia, found that the battle for quiet with our Lord became intense. Early mornings were difficult as the whole community was up with the sun after six. Late-night meetings nearly every day of the week made evenings impossible. Ill health diminished our strength, and a constant flow of visitors prevented uninterrupted times during the day. Yet how could we have known the Lord's mind for a rapidly expanding work unless we still took time to wait on him and hear his voice?

There are times when those who really love the Lord cannot be satisfied with a limited period each day. Unhurried communication with him is what we long for in our deepest hearts. In our missionary work we used to set aside days for prayer, when, alone or together in groups, we could shed any sense of rush and give ourselves to what the Westminster Confession describes so aptly as 'knowing God and enjoying him for ever'. Those who have not yet tried it cannot guess what deep enjoyment times like these can bring.

The Rev. Basil Gough was a tremendous challenge to my husband when he was in Oxford. He urged the students to make Sunday a day which is really the *Lord's*. As one possible approach he suggested an hour or so of fellowship with God before church. Missing lunch would provide a further 4 to 5 hours, when they could read devotionally, giving the Holy Spirit time to apply it personally. Praise and worship could take place with no sense of rush, and the Bible studied in far greater depth than their morning quiet times allowed. The joy of corporate worship in the evening added a good balance. These Sundays became a highlight of Martin's student days.

But not only do we need to spend time with God. We need to know how he works, and be sure of the fact that he will help us personally. Before Hudson Taylor went out to China he wanted to be sure that God was utterly reliable, that when he found himself miles away from any human aid he could know that God would not let him down. So he began to ask for definite signs of God's power to work very early on in his preparation to go to China.

Our life's work may not lie three or four months' travel away, as did Hudson Taylor's. Indeed, we may never be asked to leave home. But even so, we all need to prove God for ourselves. Each of us needs to be able to say, 'I have found that wherever I am, in whatever sort of situation, God is utterly to be trusted. He will see me through.'

The first striking answer to prayer I remember was when I was a student and was organizing the cooking at a boys' camp. At the last minute one of the assistant cooks was not able to come. We were leaving that very morning for a week's holiday in Connemara in the west of Ireland, and I prayed, 'O God, how can I ever find someone to take her place now? Please help me!' As we were picnicking some days later on an isolated beach, a car drew up and the occupants climbed out. Amazingly they turned out to be friends of my brother, and in a wonderful way the daughter, Mary, agreed to come and cook with me. Later she gave her life to the Lord at that camp. I was quite staggered at such an answer to my anxious prayer, far greater than my puny desires had ever asked for. Years later, when Martin and I found ourselves in many a difficult situation in SE Asia, I was glad that I had already begun to prove that 'God can be trusted'.

If we are to have the temerity to expect that the almighty God, the ruler of the universe, should condescend to help us with our problems, it behoves us first to examine our own hearts searchingly before him. Dare we expect him to bless us if we know we are harbouring bitterness or resentment or selfishness? Is there unwillingness in our hearts to obey God over some issue? Have we robbed someone of that which is lawfully their due time, respect, property? Is there someone we find difficult to love because temperamentally we are poles apart, yet we know full well that our Master said, 'This is my commandment, that you love one another as I have loved you' (Jn. 15:12)?

We can only expect to see the blessing of God on our lives as we are willing to expose our hearts to the searching gaze of him who has 'eyes like a flame of fire' (Rev. 1:14). We must allow him to be not only our Saviour but also our Lord. We must expect the pruning knife of the Master Gardener to work, removing the unnecessary growth and the dead branches, so that fruit for his glory will grow unimpeded (Jn. 15:2). Our great Master longs to use us, but he cannot do so without the necessary spiritual preparation.

Biblical preparation

As servants of a risen Saviour it is not our own thoughts and ideas which we bring to a needy world. Christianity is a religion based on revelation. God has not left us to grope towards him, but has revealed himself through creation, through history, through the prophets and above all through his Son. And this revelation we find in the Bible. It is therefore of the utmost importance that every one who wishes to serve God should steep themselves in the teaching of the Bible. All our beliefs and doctrinal formulations must come under the scrutiny of the Scriptures. To be able to do this the biblical scholar must be familiar not only with the better-known passages but with the whole sweep of the divine revelation.

How few Christians there are who have read the Bible from cover to cover. We follow some scheme of readings which jumps from Old Testament to New Testament and back again, missing out the more 'tedious' parts! No wonder there is little knowledge of biblical history in our churches. No wonder large parts of the Scriptures are quite unfamiliar to many Christians.

I was brought up on the Authorized Version, but there are so many readable versions of the Bible today that we really have no excuse. By all means use a more accurate version for your Bible study, but buy a modern translation as well and read it right through as if it were a novel. Begin to grasp the wonder of God's over-all plan. See how the prophets

Get Set! 49

fitted into Israel's history and sense how relevant their message was for their day. Let the rapid rise of Christianity after Pentecost enthuse your imagination and spark off a belief that God can do it again.

While stretching out after God's vast plan for the world in the over-all sweep of Scripture, there are hidden treasures too in the detailed study of individual books. We have in the English language the fruit of many centuries of biblical scholarship, and the different books of the Bible can best be studied together with a detailed commentary. The Bible Speaks Today is a very helpful series, but there are many others equally good. The knowledge of someone who can read the original Hebrew or Greek, and has spent years studying the background situation, is a tremendous asset. Perhaps up to now you have used helpful dated notes like those published by the Scripture Union or Bible Reading Fellowship. But that was the 'milk'. Move on to the 'meat' and profit by the wealth of scholarship which is available to you.

The churches in this country need men and women of God who have a thorough grasp of the teaching of the Bible. And from overseas the call comes for those who can teach and train others in the Word. It is not a superficial understanding that these Christians overseas are looking for – they also have their theologically trained leaders. During Martin's early days in Indonesia he was taken by a national pastor to a remote village, nearly a day's bus journey into the jungle, to minister to the local church over the weekend. On emerging sleepily from his bedroom the following morning and being about to make his way to the river for an early morning wash, Martin was hailed by the pastor. 'We need your help,' he called. 'The Bible teacher and I were discussing the Old Testament background to the doctrine of predestination. What do you make of it?' And Martin was expected to furnish an intelligent reply!

The servant of God requires not only a knowledge of Scripture for its own sake, but above all in order to apply it to real life situations. As a minister or youth worker in this country you will be up against many practical problems. What does the Bible teach about marriage and divorce, and how can we apply it in our rapidly crumbling society today? How can the church meet problems of loneliness, rootlessness or purposelessness in our community? What contribution does the Bible make to the debate on discipline and freedom, or violence and crime? Does the Bible have anything to say on modern-day politics?

Overseas an ability to apply the teaching of Scripture to many situational problems is a necessity. The young churches are grappling with a great diversity of key issues and need guidance in applying scriptural truths to their own context. How should they deal with all the social implications of polygamy? What should be their attitude to food offered to spirits? How does one resolve the tension between loyalty to one's own close-knit family and loyalty to Christ? How far should the church exercise discipline over its members?

These and many more practical issues call for the preparation of a deep and sensitive knowledge of the Bible. This will not grow through a cursory glance at the day's passage followed by a quick hunt for 'my thought for the day'. It requires the man or woman of God to be sufficiently disciplined to lay aside adequate time for study and meditation, to glean all they can from the findings of others and prayerfully to seek the Holy Spirit's illumination of his own inspired word.

Personal discipline

If you have read this far you will not be surprised that personal discipline is our next topic! Discipline is not a popular word today. 'Freedom' and 'self-expression' are far more to the current taste. Yet you will search the Bible in vain to find an exhortation to 'do your own thing'. The whole tenor of Scripture is one of order. Children are to obey their parents and slaves their masters. Church members should yield to the persuasion of their elders. Wives should submit to their husbands and all of us to each other – and above all we are to submit to Christ. And Christ already demonstrates the perfect freedom to be found in a life of complete obedience to his Father. There are those today who are slaves to freedom, not knowing that true freedom is found only in being a slave to Christ.

Our Master has called his servants to a life of discipline and obedience. The last part of the fruit of the Spirit (and therefore perhaps the climax?) is self-control. This must be the aim of everyone who is attempting to prepare for effective service for God.

In one of his earlier letters, written from the thick of the pressures of a demanding missionary life, Paul wrote: 'I do not run aimlessly, I do not box as one beating the air, but I pommel my body and subdue it' (1 Cor. 9:26–27). Here we have a glimpse into the secret as to how this little man of insignificant stature could survive a life of incredible hardship. (Read prayerfully his own testimony in 2 Cor. 11:23–28.) Humanly speaking the answer lies in the fact that Paul was tough. He never pampered his body. He had learnt to sleep anywhere, eat anything, carry on in spite of everything. He knew what self-discipline meant.

In writing to his special trainee, Timothy, Paul uses the illustration of the hard-working farmer who deserves first share of the crops, the athlete who is crowned only as a result of long discipline and the soldier on active service who cannot afford to allow himself to be entangled by civilian pursuits (2 Tim. 2:4–6). The implication comes to us all to master the art of hard work and personal discipline. We have a duty to God to keep his gift to us of our bodies as trim and as fit as possible. Daily exercise is not an unspiritual waste of time. If our bodies are fit we are more likely to last longer in demanding circumstances. Many Bible College students discipline themselves to go jogging each day or to do fitness exercises. Sensible sleep patterns form an essential part of the Christian's life. You cannot stay up until the early hours of the morning and then expect to be fresh early next day to meet with your Master. It is costly to take yourself off to bed when all your friends are still laughing and chatting; but if you mean business for

God he will give you the courage to do it. If you were training for the Olympics your friends would understand. Tell them you are training for something greater!

With an eye to the practical, Paul gives us a brief exhortation, 'eat whatever is set before you' (1 Cor. 10:27). We sometimes wished we could put this up in the dining room when Martin and I were in charge of the orientation of a continual stream of new missionaries in Singapore. It is extraordinary how fussy some people can be over what they eat. This may not cause too many problems in their own home, though their parents or future partner could well be exasperated by it. In a foreign culture it is the height of bad manners not to be able to eat, and hopefully to enjoy, whatever they go to the trouble of serving. I have always worked on the principle that if someone else likes some food I can learn to like it too, and brought my children up that they must have at least one mouthful of every dish, whether they like it or not. It is amazing how the taste for something can develop. And horrifying how a charming hostess can be hurt by the fact that you cannot touch fat, or never take curry, or appear reluctant to sample her delicious dishes.

Many of us need to watch our own private self-indulgence. Are we the sort who cannot stop buying things when we see them, whether we need them or not? Some waste money over numerous paperbacks, or make-up, or CD's, or women's magazines. None of these things are wrong; but is something becoming an obsession in our life? We need to ask ourselves: 'If I were to be called to tribal work in the

Andes where I could no longer buy this particular thing, how badly would I miss it?' What about cutting down on it now to prove to yourself that you can do without it? If the money saved is given to some specific Christian work you will be able to thank God that you are taking the first steps towards learning the meaning of sacrifice for his sake.

Finance is a matter in which all of us can afford to learn discipline. The western world is full of those who have far too much and think they have far too little. Anyone who doubts this need only pay a visit to a third-world country and see what they have to manage to live on. The pressures of a materialistic age unconsciously mould us into thinking that luxuries are necessities. The best antidote to the desire to keep up with the Joneses is to sit down and work out, 'If I were to forgo my new hi-fi (or hairdrier or gadget for the car) how many gallons of paraffin would it buy so that my missionary friends would no longer have to cook on wood? How many Bibles would it purchase, or courses of anti-leprosy treatment?' The things which mop up our money so often are mere accessories, not the basic essentials which so many others need.

The early Christians counted it a privilege to be able to give to the Lord's work. The young church in Jerusalem experienced a spontaneous sharing of all their possessions, so that 'no one said that any of the things which he possessed was his own, but they had everything in common' (Acts 4:32). The new converts in Philippi sent love gifts to assist Paul when he was forced to leave them so hurriedly (Phil. 4:14–16).

Their actions demonstrated a joy in giving, a delight in being able to share with their brothers and sisters in Christ. It was not a miserly or coldly calculated attitude, but one which sprang from their deep sense of gratitude to God and sharing in the Lord's work. They knew 'the grace of our Lord Jesus Christ, that though he was rich, yet for (their) sake he became poor' (2 Cor. 8:9), and their thankfulness found its outlet in giving: 'not reluctantly, or under compulsion, for God loves a cheerful giver' (2 Cor. 9:7).

The Old Testament standard was that every Jew must give a tenth of all their income. This was automatically assumed. On top of that they were then free to give their love gifts as well. One of the reasons why the Christian church today is so short of money is that her members have not learnt the joy of generous giving. As the Lord prompts us to pour our resources into the work of his kingdom, we shall discover the truth of his words, 'It is more blessed to give than to receive.'

If you are thinking of a life-time's service for God you will need to face the possibility of several years' training. Bible and missionary colleges cost money and it would be well to begin saving up for this expense. While teaching I lived frugally in order to save up for Bible College. I was amazed at how cheaply I could live even without skimping on the basic essentials, and at how quickly my bank balance grew.

Tidiness is another matter over which some will need to practise personal discipline. Two missionaries in an isolated situation can easily find the tension mounting between them if one is persistently untidy or the other excessively tidy. The same applies to flatmates in this country, or to husbands and wives! A little true Christian *agapē* will aim to make life easy for the other person as far as possible.

Personal relationships

Here lies an area which presents the biggest obstacle to full-time service for many people. It is relatively easy to master the art of addressing a room full of people, but far harder to hold meaningful relationships with each one present.

The secure framework of society in western countries is crumbling around us, so that many young people are still groping after their own identity and worth, and may have difficulty in reaching out to others. Individuals whose home circumstances have caused much pain and bruising, can find much of their energy absorbed in working through their own problems. Until they begin to come to terms with their own reactions and their own background, their ministry to others will be hampered.

The tragedies hidden in so many homes today are bound to leave their scars on the new generation. Yet the miracle of the gospel shows us that God can bring 'beauty out of ashes'. The Creator God, who was able to bring the highest good out of the greatest tragedy in the history of the world, can yet bring good out of human suffering today. As a child I was separated for five years from my missionary parents because of the war, and then my own mother died. For years I was baffled at what God had allowed to happen to me. 'Surely I would have been a more complete and whole person,' I argued with myself, 'if I had had a normal family life!' But God has gently had to show me that there are certain flowers which will only bloom in very arid conditions. It was only as I came to terms with myself that I found a real care for others developing. The very bruises and hurts which God has allowed in our lives can produce a quickened sensitivity to the needs of others and a greater awareness as to how to meet them.

Those who are preparing for Christian ministry of any kind need to take time to face up to themselves honestly and objectively. Before they can help others they need to begin to understand how they themselves react, what sparks them off, what makes them clam up. In the knowledge of their own hearts they will find the key to the understanding of others.

We are all aware of certain people with whom we have a natural affinity and others to whom we relate with more difficulty. It is important that the Christian worker should be able to mix happily with people of all sorts. It can be exciting learning to bridge the generation gap, learning to appreciate the greater wisdom and maturity of older people, even if they do seem a bit old-fashioned. Friendship across the generations can bring great joy. And it is a help when considering the immaturity of some younger person to remember that we were floundering just like that only five years ago!

It is human nature to want to associate with people who think as we do. We all naturally gravitate towards those with our own educational or cultural background. But as a minister in this country, or a missionary overseas, you will be required to relate to people of all types. My husband and I have found in the college where we teach that the rich diversity in the student body is a vital element in training for ministry. Some have never mixed with people outside their own community. John, a warm-hearted, burly window cleaner, was put in charge of one of the church teams. Rosy was one of his team-members. Unknown to him she had an MA in theology. They worked together very happily until one day John discovered Rosy's qualifications. 'If I'd known you had an MA I wouldn't have had you in my team,' he burst out, suddenly feeling very inferior. Rosy laughed. They were both learning to relate with someone from a completely different background from their own.

Our children had the advantage of being brought up in the multi-racial city of Singapore, and find little difficulty in mixing with people of any race. But many feel shy in the presence of someone with a different-coloured skin. 'What shall I talk about?' they wonder. The only way to overcome this is deliberately to put yourself where you will meet with people of other nationalities. Do things together, listen to their conversation, try and stand in their shoes and see how they are feeling. If you are truly interested in them they will forgive a few bricks dropped in the early days, providing your genuine love shines through.

People who are preparing for Christian ministry should make a point of going to situations where they will meet all sorts of people. You need to be able to mix with ease with the wealthy and the poor, the refined and the more uncouth, the cultured and the less educated. It is one of the tragedies of the church in this country that it mainly penetrates the middle strata of society and largely leaves untouched the two extremes. We need those who, for the love of Christ, can love everyone from whatever background, mixing easily and making real friendships. Ask yourself whether you gravitate only to those of your own kind.

Overseas the expatriate community is very small and you may have to live at close quarters with others from a very different background from yours. In this country you may choose your flatmates, but there the situation will dictate who lives with you, and who shares your day off. The ability to master the problems of personal relationships may be one of the most influential factors in keeping you at your post overseas.

Experience

I have the privilege of sitting on a missionary society's selection panel. One of the first questions I would want to ask an intending candidate is, 'What experience have you had already? What are you qualified to do?' Service for God is not an escape channel. Those selecting candidates for the ministry are looking for people who have already faced the rough and tumble of life. Theological study alone will not equip us adequately for a pastoral ministry. Do you long to serve God? Prove your calibre by undergoing the discipline of a secular training. The completion of a course with full qualifications at the end is a necessary part to character training. The mental discipline that develops the skills learnt will shape your personality, forming the underlying strength and maturity which will be necessary in later years.

It is good to remember that God wishes us to train for something we can do well and enjoy, not just the profession we feel we ought to enter. But we should not be content with merely scraping through. Whatever we do is to be done to the glory of God (1 Cor. 10:31), and our studies fall into this category too. It is a poor witness when the members of a college Christian Union are so busy having fellowship together that their academic work suffers. How many people in the third world would dearly love the privilege we have of training!

In today's demanding circumstances a basic qualification may not be adequate. Ask yourself whether there are further qualifications which would be useful. For instance, if you are training as a State Registered Nurse, should the midwifery diploma be your next step? Few missionary hospitals would be satisfied with the basic SRN. They need nurses with wider experience who can supervise wards or be sister tutors. The national nurses do the everyday work on the wards.

Many of our western qualifications are largely academic. Some years in secular work will help us to consolidate our knowledge and apply it to real life situations. Our Lord spent thirty years in training before he started his ministry. He worked with his hands as a carpenter to make a living for his mother and younger brothers and sisters. He learnt how to deal with complaints and criticism from his customers. He rubbed shoulders with the neighbours and knew who needed humouring and who was hungry for a word of encouragement. He knew the urgent problem of trying to make both ends meet when serving an impoverished community, none of whom could afford to pay liberally for work done. As we read the Gospel accounts we are aware of Christ's amazing insight into people's hearts. Humanly speaking he developed this during those 'hidden years' when he was up against all the problems of everyday life, seeking his heavenly Father's guidance on how to cope with each situation.

Together with professional and secular work comes the need to gain experience in as many forms of Christian service as possible. When we worked in Indonesia my husband and I were called upon to start a youth fellowship, train Sunday school teachers, teach Religious Education in schools and colleges, preach in village and city churches, lead evangelistic teams, take leadership training courses and guide the development of the work among women. How thankful we were for every kind of Christian service we had practised before leaving England.

You may feel, 'I am going overseas as an agricultural adviser, or a doctor. There is no need for me to be able to speak at meetings.' But the nationals to whom we minister know nothing of our western dichotomy between the sacred and the secular. For them, religion saturates every side of life. They need to see what Christ means to you as you plant out the cabbages or empty a patient's bedpan. A brief talk given by the doctor who has operated on them will be far more telling because of the fact that they are already indebted to you. The demonstration of your Christian love in practical ways will gain a hearing for the speaking skills which you must set yourself to develop now.

If you have already done some Sunday School teaching why not offer to help with the Youth Fellowship for a while, or a home Bible study group? Tremendous joy can be found in visiting an old people's home. There are many weak, sick and elderly people who need the Lord's love just as much as one's own vivacious contemporaries. Have you always lived among middle-class folk? Get the bus down to the city centre and lend a hand at the club there. Or perhaps God is wanting you to learn to preach, but there would be few opportunities in your own well-organized church. Find out if there are any small chapels in your area. They might well be thankful for your youthful help and your own church can do without you once a month. It is much easier to begin a speaking career in a small group where you are not known!

Visiting is a ministry which many young people avoid. 'I wouldn't know what to say!' But how then would you manage if you found yourself in some African or Asian town where your white skin and faltering attempt at the language make you stick out like a sore thumb? Much better to begin to practise in your own culture and your own mother tongue. Why not plan door-to-door visiting for some special meeting and go along with someone who has done it before? The Lord, who promised to tell Moses what to say, will be with you and he will give you the words. Many elderly people and other 'shut-ins' appreciate a call from a young person, provided you are sensitive to their feelings and respect them as people. It can be exciting attempting something new for the Lord. You may never know you have a gift until you start to exercise it, and the Lord delights in giving us a lovely surprise. I wonder if the tough herdsman Amos, caring for his goats outside the Judean village of Tekoa, was surprised to discover he had the gift of prophecy?

There is much to be learnt too about the organization of a church. Who cleans the gutters when they become clogged with leaves, and whose responsibility is it to notice dry rot setting in? How does a minister manage to keep in touch with each of his several hundred members? Is he directly in touch with all, or does he delegate responsibility? Which jobs can be delegated in a church? Which jobs could be, but are not? What oils the wheels of your church, and how are problems ironed out?

All this implies the need for a genuine commitment to a home church. The fluid society in which we live often hinders the development of church links, but they are important. Many students are converted at college, and their Christian Union is regarded as a substitute for a church. But whether you are going into the ministry at home or overseas you will need a home church to stand behind you. Their spiritual support and their prayers may make all the difference in the years to come.

Yet it should not just be 'all take' on our part. Here and now is your chance to give to the fellowship. As you really pull your weight in the community of your church, bearing responsibility, caring and sharing, the ties will strengthen. They will begin to feel that you truly are their own missionary or minister in training and will follow your development with spiritual concern.

Much valuable experience may be gained through several months spent with the organizations mentioned already, like Operation Mobilisation or Youth with a Mission. Here there will be training sessions interspersed with opportunities for service. You will be expected to help with literature work, door-to-door visiting, chatting to people on the streets, talking about the Lord anywhere and everywhere and learning how to lead someone to Christ.

Saturdays or some weeks of holiday spent helping in the local Christian bookshop can be greatly enriching. Many people come in for a chat because they are lonely or need advice, and the Lord can show you how to encourage or guide them as you recommend a helpful book.

During the holiday months large numbers of camps are organized by various Christian groups. These can be great times of tremendous fun coupled with spiritual growth as we share with and learn from the others. My first lessons in children's work came from helping with a beach mission in Perranporth when I was in my teens. I shall never forget the high standards the leaders set for the meetings: plenty of interest and variety, with excellent content and relevant teaching.

A number of missionary societies organize a short-term helpers' scheme where volunteers go out for a limited time. Here is the opportunity to live with missionaries and learn from working with them, and yet to be able to contribute in some way through the skills which God has given you. A period spent in this way provides a good chance of seeing some of the opportunities and problems of missionary life. Through a limited time like this God has often confirmed a call to missionary work, or developed a prayerful concern for this other country which will enrich both parties.

A period with VSO or a similar organization could provide comparable opportunities. The lack of Christian fellowship, however, may lead to a far less congenial situation, and an inexperienced Christian may find it very tough going.

It is greatly encouraging to know that God has his plans for our time of preparation just as much as for our future work. Here is another chance to learn to discern the will of the Lord and to obey him gladly.

Information

We live in an age of highly developed communication. News of happenings anywhere in the world floods our papers. Informative talks and perceptive discussions on many different countries form part of our radio and TV programmes. It is possible to go to a public library and borrow books on almost any part of the world or any stratum of society. With the advent of the Internet, a wealth of information lies at our finger-tips waiting for the alert enquirer to unearth.

If we feel called to a full-time ministry there is much we can do to prepare for it by finding out beforehand all we can. Perhaps the Lord is leading to ordination in this country. Are you finding out about the role of your own denomination in our nation's life? There are rich libraries on its history, its development, its position in the nation-wide church. Have we begun to assess the historical backgrounds of our various denominations and to learn from Christians of other traditions? Many analyses have been done on what makes churches grow. Why is it that one church may be increasing steadily, numerically and spiritually, whereas a neighbouring church faces a hard up-hill struggle? A grave problem today is the church in an inner-city situation. Can these churches expect to see growth?

Perhaps God is leading you towards more specialist work, say among teenagers. Their fashions and tastes change so quickly that it is important that we keep ourselves informed as to what appeals to them. Looking through the magazines they enjoy or occasionally watching 'Top of the Pops' can be helpful. Magazines, books and training conferences are offered to us by groups like Scripture Union, the Church Pastoral Aid Society and Crusaders, and should be used to the full.

Preparation for work among immigrants calls for a great deal of study. They have all come from countries rich in their own traditions and folklore. Although mostly English-speaking now, many of them still keep their own customs and tenaciously

Get Set!

cling to their own religion. A sensitive understanding of their feelings and a deep appreciation of their traditions will go far towards making us acceptable as friends.

It is helpful to look out for programmes on radio and television which deal with the problems of immigrants. Travel films often reveal something of their way of living and their outlook on life. The study of other people's religions may be fascinating and challenging, even though at first some of their concepts are difficult to grasp. Our western objective and pragmatic view of life stands in sharp contrast to the Asian mystical approach. The West Indian, on the other hand, comes from a background steeped in high-church Anglicanism. Their love of colour and rhythm has opened the way for the mushrooming of black Pentecostal churches.

The need for well-informed knowledge applies as well to the Christian worker preparing to go overseas. Maybe you are still at the very early stages and have little idea where God wants you to work. You can start by getting in touch with one or two missionary societies and taking their magazines. As your knowledge grows through prayerful reading of each issue you will begin to discern the strategy behind their various objectives and sense for yourself whether this is a group you could happily work with. Gradually a picture will build up about the area they work in, the people and their customs, and the strengths and weaknesses of the national church.

Linking with missionaries in prayer can be an enriching experience. As you follow their progress through their letters and sensitively stand alongside them in prayer, a deepening bond can form between the two of you. God may clarify his will for you through such times of prayer.

With a growing interest in a particular missionary society, it may be helpful to attend some of their conferences. These can be tremendously valuable times when we set aside the pressures of everyday life and focus on the work of God in some other country. The lively talks and discussion groups can give new insights into the overseas situation, providing a far deeper understanding of the opportunities and problems involved. Time for relaxed conversation over meals with different missionaries can be greatly beneficial, with the chance to ask the questions you could not bring up in a public meeting.

Attending a missionary conference is a good way of finding out the particular ethos of that society. Each mission is different and has its own characteristics. The organizational structure varies enormously, as does the way finance is handled. There will be many questions you may want to ask concerning personnel matters, authority within the mission, provision for missionaries' children, length of terms, etc. The Lord can use all this to confirm to you whether or not this is the society with which he wishes you to work.

In recent years a growing number of more realistically honest missionary books have been published. The swing away from the Victorian climate of turning a missionary into almost a 'super-saint' has accompanied the realization that missionaries are human just like everyone else. Your insight into missionary situations will increase enormously as you make time to read some of these biographies. Books dealing with the historical development of the overseas church can help to give objective perspectives too.

If you feel the Lord has shown you clearly what area of the world you will be working in, there is much you can do to read about the background of this country. The public library should provide access to its history, geography, ethnic races, economy and politics. We need to have formed a clear picture of the over-all situation before we can grasp where the heart needs of the people lie and think through how Jesus Christ can meet those needs.

There are also many lessons to be learnt on missionary strategy. Our mass media have made it popular to criticize the image of the Victorian missionary, forcing western 'civilization' on to their converts as an integral part of their evangelistic fervour. This picture may well be a caricature of the truth, though it would be foolish to deny that we are children of our own age and each generation has its glaring faults. How important it is, then, that we should study the mistakes and successes of our predecessors and think through what we can learn from them. The person intending to go overseas, whether in a secular job or as a missionary, cannot afford to omit studying missionary strategy.

As the Lord lays on your heart a growing concern for the world-wide spread of his kingdom you may well feel that you wish to form a small prayer-group. Here several dedicated people can gather for urgent intercessory prayer. If each one is linked with a different missionary or full-time worker in this country, you can pool your information about their prayer needs and share in each other's concern. The personal link with individual workers can make a great difference. We are all *human*, and as such our hearts warm to *people*, not to societies. With growing knowledge of their hopes and fears, imaginative, caring prayer can be part of our on-going relationship.

This will lead on to a closer involvement, part of which will be a growing realization of our responsibility to give. Real love cannot help but give. As our knowledge of the spreading of God's kingdom world-wide grows, and our concern deepens, the Lord can clearly show how this should be expressed in practical terms.

Training

As a keen young Christian with a fair amount of Bible knowledge and some experience, one longs to be on the job, actively serving the Lord. But all denominations and missions consider Bible training essential for the future Christian worker.

The years of preparation can often feel irksome and unnecessarily long. Yet we know well that in the secular world no post of great responsibility is reached without extensive training. Hasty or slipshod preparation for any task can only result in poor-quality work.

If the Lord is leading towards ordination in this country, your own denomination may want you to go to a denominational college. In the Anglican Church the vicar will doubtless refer you to the Diocesan

Director of Ordinands through whom you will be put in contact with the Advisory Council for the Church's Ministry. The Church Pastoral Aid Society can give further help through its excellent 'You and the Ministry' weekends. With their wide experience and contact their advice is freely available for all who are considering the ministry. For the Baptist ministry you need to be recommended by your own church and partially supported by them while you study at a college recognized by the Baptist Union. Similarly, other denominations have their own channels to which your minister can refer you.

Many colleges which used to prepare ministers for their own denominations alone now take students on a much wider basis. For example, one College training for the Anglican ministry has both Methodists and Baptists among its teaching staff and a proportion of non-Anglican students, some of whom are training for the ministry in their own churches. This is not unique among denominational colleges. Most Bible colleges have for years demonstrated the reality of Christian unity by transcending denominational boundaries.

Colleges vary considerably. Some provide courses which are largely geared to the home ministry or to teaching religious education. Others train particularly for service overseas. Some colleges are fairly heavily booked and the intending student may need to apply well in advance. Writing for information does not commit you: the doors will not open automatically. In fact, if a college pushes you to come without adequate screening, warning lights should be flashing in your mind!

Some people wonder if they could do their training through the excellent Bible correspondence courses available, rather than having to become full-time students again. Much benefit can be gained through these courses, but they are of necessity largely academic. One of the values of attending a Bible college is that training takes place in a community. The students will learn to sort through their problems in a group situation, where other people's very different experience will shed new light on their own. Fellowship with others of like mind can be tremendously enriching and lead to life-long friendships. The opportunity will be given for guided service in teams with others, where each member can contribute and receive. The college will provide opportunities to hear key Christian workers from all types of ministry, with the accompanying challenge to rethink our approaches and to revitalize our faith as to what God can do today.

In choosing a college for training for Christian service it is helpful to look at the relationship between the academic and the practical. The college should have high academic standards, but should also be thoroughly practical and relevant to the future sphere of ministry. There should be no dichotomy between the practical and academic, and no undue emphasis on one above the other.

Attitudes both at home and overseas are changing rapidly, so that some have said that a new generation arises every five years. It is important therefore to choose a college which is really up-to-date, and constantly re-appraising its course in the light of fresh situations. The training even for ten years ago will not do for today. We also live in what has been termed a 'global village', with large population movements and the bringing together of many different races. Those preparing to work in this country, as well as those going abroad, need to study Islam and eastern religions, and think through how to present Christ in an attractive and relevant manner to each of these communities.

In our future ministry we shall give not only our knowledge, but ourselves. There is a real need for individual tutoring and counselling at every level throughout the college so that the whole personality is trained. We should be looking for an atmosphere where the staff are readily available to the students, and in close relationship with them.

The importance of going to a college which will provide a thoroughly biblical training cannot be over-stressed. There are many Christian institutions which substitute human reason and human theories for the revealed Word of God. Of course it is important to know theological trends, both in past history and the current ones of today. But the uniqueness of Christianity lies in the fact that it is God seeking us, not us seeking God. The Almighty Creator God has revealed himself to us through his Son, made known to us in the Word of God. Everything necessary for faith and salvation is found here. Intending Christian workers need a college which will guide them into developing a clear biblical faith, and the ability to handle the Scriptures in evangelism and effective biblical exposition and application.

Above all, the college chosen should be one which will challenge and deepen the student's own walk with God. He is the one we are serving. If we know him only dimly and sense his will only imperfectly, how can we hope to have an effective ministry? All the other training is useless apart from the spiritual side. We may have a wide biblical knowledge and be trained in perfect techniques, and yet find that our work for the Lord is powerless. The miracle of a new birth is an act which God alone can bring about. The growth of a church comes only through the work of God. 'Neither he who plants nor he who waters is anything, but only God who gives the growth' (1 Cor. 3:6).

Every college has its own ethos and emphases. Write to several colleges asking for their syllabus and other literature, and try to get a feel of their particular slant. Meeting some of the students they have turned out can be a great help, providing opportunity to ask more detailed questions. Your own minister or the leaders of the missionary society in which you are interested should be able to advise you as well. If the Lord is wanting you in full-time service for him, he will have just the right college in which you can train.

3

Go!

When Martin and I were new missionaries working in Indonesia, one day a weather-beaten farmer stood shyly by our door. The sarong which he wore was faded and shabby, his hands were gnarled from years of manual labour. He hesitated to enter a foreigner's home; but there was something he was burning to tell us.

With a glass of hot sweet tea in his hands he gradually lost his embarrassment, and after some encouragement he told us why he had come.

'I live in the village of...' he began. 'All my life has been empty. I worked hard and did what I thought was right but it was all purposeless.'

Gathering confidence he continued. 'It was as if all my life I had been climbing a tree and searching its branches for fruit. Climb as high as I could and search as I would, I found nothing. Then you came to our village and told us about Jesus Christ. As I listened I realized that here was the fruit I was looking for. So I scrambled down and started to climb up the tree of Jesus Christ. I don't mind how difficult it is or how many scratches I get on the way. I've found fruit which satisfies.'

In his simple way that Indonesian farmer expressed a very profound truth. Life for the non-Christian is empty. They may pretend to be happy, satisfied and successful. But now and again the mask drops, revealing the hollow emptiness inside.

You and I hold the answer to their searching. You and I know the only solution which will meet their heartache. How can we keep the glorious news of the gospel of Jesus Christ to ourselves? How dare we ignore the world's glaring needs and its cries for help?

The Holy Spirit is moving today in a new way in many areas. Parts of Indonesia have seen huge increases in church membership and mass baptisms where up to a thousand people have been baptized in one day. The Pentecostal churches in Latin America have seen phenomenal growth in the past decades. Young Christians are active in street evangelism; daughter congregations are springing up sweeping crowds of new city-dwellers into the church. Parts of Africa have seen steady continuous revival for over a generation and other African churches are experiencing a great release of new life and power.

In many parts of the world the Holy Spirit is at work. Are we content to stand on the sideline and refuse to be involved? What about the needs of all these thousands of new Christians for biblical teaching, spiritual guidance and pastoral care as they face the perplexing problems of today's world?

As we all know, there are other areas where the progress of the gospel is stifled. Greed, selfishness and injustice leave tragedy in their wake. Indifference and apathy have made people's hearts cold to the love of God.

The solution to any problem lies with the individual. We have no right to say 'they' ought to be doing something about it. God's challenge comes: Don't look at others, look at yourself. All the great movements in Christian history have come about through one individual who has been obedient to the call of God, and stepped out in faith regardless of where it will lead. The movements have grown through other individuals who have responded and said, 'I want to be part of God's on-going work. I, too, am willing to put God first and follow him whatever it may involve.'

The call of God comes to each of us. What am I personally doing about Christ's last specific command: 'You are to go into all the world and preach the Good News to everyone, everywhere'?

Resources

Books:

Missionary Methods – St Paul's or Ours? Roland Allen (Eerdmans)

*Introduction to the Science of Missions J H Bavinck (Presbyterian and Reformed, Philadelphia)

Understanding Church Growth D McGavran (Eerdmans)

God Can Be Trusted Elizabeth Goldsmith (Overseas Missionary Fellowship)

Life's Tapestry Martin Goldsmith (OM)

Cinderella with Amnesia Michael Griffiths (Inter-Varsity Press)

Give up your Small Ambitions Michael Griffiths (Inter-Varsity Press)

Day by Day Guidance Paul Little (Falcon)

History of Christian Missions Stephen Neill (Pelican)

*Discipling the Nations R DeRidder (Baker Book House)

*Christian Mission in the Modern World John Stott (Falcon)

Biography of Hudson Taylor Dr and Mrs Howard Taylor (Overseas Missionary Fellowship)
Who'd be a vicar? Robin Toley (Falcon)
You and the ministry ed. Robin Toley (Falcon)

* indicates more advanced books

Organizations:

The Salmon Youth Centre in Bermondsey, 43 Old Jamaica Road, London SE16 4TE

Church Pastoral Aid Society, Athena Drive, Tachbrook Park, Warwick, CV34 6NG

Counties, 30 Haynes Road, Westbury, BA13 3HD

Crusaders Union, 2 Romeland Hill, St Albans, Herts, AL3 4ET

Echoes of Service, 1 Widcombe Crescent, Bath, BA2 6AQ

International Fellowship of Evangelical Students (IFES Trust International Office), 55 Palmerston Road, Wealdstone, Harrow, HA3 7RR

Interserve, 325 Kennington Road, London SE11 4QH

Mayflower Family Centre, Vincent Street, London E16 1LZ

The Navigators, Adyar House, 32 Carlton Crescent, Southampton, SO15 2EW

Newham Community Renewal Programme Ltd., 170 Harold Road, Plaistow, London E13 0SE

Oasis Trust, 115 Southwark Bridge Road, London, SE1 0AX

OMF International (UK), Station Approach, Borough Green, Sevenoaks, TN15 8BG

Operation Mobilisation, The Quinta, Western Rhyn, Oswestry, SY10 7LT

Scripture Union, 207 Queensway, Bletchley, Milton Keynes, MK2 2EB

Tearfund, 100 Church Road, Teddington, Middlesex, TW11 8QE

WEC International, Bulstrode, Oxford Road, Gerrards Cross, SL9 8SZ

Youth For Christ, PO Box 5254, Halesowen, B63 3DG

Youth With A Mission UK (YWAM), Highfield Oval, Ambrose Lane, Harpenden, AL5 4BX

Names and addresses of colleges and missionary societies are obtainable from Evangelical Alliance, Whitefield House, 186 Kennington Park Road, London SE11 4BT.

Vacational Activities, produced by UCCF, 38 De Montfort Street, Leicester LE1 7GP.

For a full list of organizations see the UK Christian Handbook

Kingdom Life

Martin Goldsmith

*To Elizabeth
my much-loved wife
and joyful companion,
unfailing in her encouragement,
gentle in her criticism,
a perceptive editor.*

Contents

Foreword	85
1 The Kingdom	87
2 It's God's Kingdom	97
3 Entering the Kingdom	111
4 Kingdom Life	122
5 It Has Come, It Will Come	143
Questions for Discussion	151
Bibliography	154

Foreword

The modern reader of the New Testament may be surprised to find John the Baptist and Jesus starting their preached message with the announcement that 'the kingdom of heaven is at hand' (Matt. 3:2; 4:17) without any explanation of what they mean by the expression 'kingdom of heaven'. Clearly they assumed a widespread knowledge of the traditional Jewish understanding of the kingdom.

Christians today lack that background of rabbinic teaching; so we easily fall into wrong ideas about the life of the kingdom. While there are various solid theological works to guide the expert on this subject, it seems that we need careful biblical expositions of the kingdom in popular form, for we are assailed by the left and right wings of evangelicalism on this topic.

Is the kingdom life particularly evidenced by signs and wonders plus vibrant worship and close-knit church life? Or is 'the kingdom' shorthand for a passionate concern for social justice? Or is it intimately connected to repentance and holiness with humility?

How did Jesus and John the Baptist picture the kingdom life?

These burning issues are hot potatoes in the church today. They are also central to the message of the New Testament itself. The gospels and the teaching of Jesus are based on the message of the kingdom. The epistles continue to some extent that central teaching of kingdom life, but concentrate more on the king of the kingdom, Jesus Christ himself. He is Lord of all. In any biblical Christian teaching and in all true kingdom living Jesus Christ our Lord must be centre-stage. In this book we shall attempt to examine some of these fundamental questions about the kingdom, but we must not allow our quest for kingdom life to displace the person and work of Jesus Christ from his central position. Let him be praised, honoured, served and loved!

1

The Kingdom

'Repent, for the kingdom of heaven is at hand' (Matt. 3:2). Dressed in camel skins and eating only locusts and wild honey, John the Baptist burst on to the stage of history. He flouted all the fads of fashion, but people flocked out from the city into the wilderness to hear his message. Among the crowds was Jesus himself, who then began his ministry with the same words – 'Repent, for the kingdom of heaven is at hand' (Matt. 4:17).

To all outward appearances Jesus was just like all the others in the crowd, but actually this was the King of kings breaking into world history to inaugurate the kingdom of God on earth. As we shall see, this would contrast sharply with the world's values: God's rule is radical, with its totally different goals and lifestyle.

At first Jesus did not explain what he meant by 'the kingdom of God'. In the coming months he would fill in many of the details of his vision. But he was also aware that his audience had considerable background understanding of the kingdom from their knowledge of the Old Testament and the traditional teaching of the rabbis.

The Jews had such rich experience of God as king. Life as slaves in Egypt was hopeless and demoralising – and then God had stepped in to deliver them from the might of Pharaoh. He overwhelmed the Egyptians with his amazing miracles and finally slaughtered all the first-born babies in Egypt. Pharaoh was quick to let them go after that! Then the Egyptian army chased Israel to bring them back into slavery. But God drowned the lot in the Red Sea. He marched in a pillar of cloud and fire before the Israelites (the kings of the surrounding nations also marched at the head of their people). Like the kings of other nearby peoples God also encamped right in their midst. He provided for them all they needed as they journeyed through the interminable barren wilderness, finally bringing them joyfully across the river Jordan into the promised land.

The divine king is always gracious and mighty. Now, as the crowds listened to Jesus, they wondered, 'Will God still do such things for his people? In ruling over us, will he deliver us, give us victory, dwell in our midst, provide for us, bring us safely into the promised new heaven and new earth?'

But years ago, after some time in the promised land their forefathers had demanded, 'appoint for us a king to govern us like all the nations' (1 Sam. 8:5). What a fearful request from a people who had known *God* as their king! It was a treacherous and rebellious decision to choose a mere human king to rule over them. No wonder God said to Samuel, 'they have rejected me from being king over them'

(1 Sam. 8:7). In their desire for authoritative human leadership like the surrounding heathen nations they turned their backs on the kingly rule of God. Saul, David and the other kings were poor substitutes for God as king.

In the Old Testament it is clear too that God not only rules over his own people Israel but also over all the nations. Pharaoh, Nebuchadnezzar, Cyrus and others thought they had power. Pride can easily go to the head of powerful world leaders! But actually God rules over them all, determining the rise and fall of empires. He also judges the nations for their sins, so the prophets have long chapters declaring 'woe' to Edom, Moab and others.

Memories of their past history will have raced through the minds of the listening crowds when they heard both John and Jesus preaching about the kingdom of God. What John introduced, Jesus takes much further.

He elaborates the theme of the kingdom particularly in the Sermon on the Mount (Matt. 5–7), shattering normal ideas of how to run a society. His ideals seem impossible. This radical sermon starts with the so-called Beatitudes. These begin and end with the kingdom. Who are the key people in the kingdom of God? People of powerful faith? Religious leaders? No! The poor in spirit and the meek, those who mourn and who hunger and thirst for righteousness, the merciful, the pure in heart, the peacemakers and those who are persecuted for righteousness' sake and for Jesus.

Jesus' teaching on kingdom life still shocks us today.

'Tremendous worship!' 'A wonderful time of prayer!' 'Brilliant fellowship!' 'Lord, Lord, we love you.' Jesus pulls us up short by saying that such things are not the true life of the kingdom. The kingdom, he says, is not found in pious people saying 'Lord, Lord' or in 'religious' experiences but in obediently doing the will of God the Father (Matt. 7:21). Such obedience is the rock-like foundation for a true kingdom life; everything else is unstable sand (Matt. 7:24–27). Kingdom life will not be seen in how we worship, but in whether we hear Jesus' words and do them (Matt. 7:24). This is God's purpose for all those who recognise Jesus as king and enter his kingdom. It is not surprising that we read that the crowds were astonished at Jesus' teaching (Matt. 7:28). It is radical!

Some Christians today feel it is right to present a brutally clear message of the gospel. Jesus was not like that. Understanding that people needed help to grasp the new values, he used parables for everyday life so that those with spiritually open ears would hear, but the hard of heart would not understand. To grasp the secrets of the kingdom is a spiritual gift (Matt. 13:11). To those whose ears and eyes are opened, more will be given in the continuously growing life of the kingdom (Matt. 13:12).

The kingdom parables

The sower (Matt. 13:3–8, 18–23; Mk. 4:3–8, 14–20)

Every Sunday school child knows this story of the seed that fell on the path, on rocky ground, among thorns and in good soil. The seed is the message of the kingdom. Some hearers are so hard-hearted that the word has no entry into their minds or hearts. Some receive it joyfully but lack the perseverance to endure through times of persecution or difficulty. Others receive the word, but it proves unfruitful because of their 'delight in riches' (Mk. 4:19). We cannot grow in the kingdom life when 'the cares of the world' (Mk. 4:19) rival the Lord for supremacy in our lives. God longs for those who will 'hear the word and understand it' (Matt. 13:23) – we notice here the importance of the spoken word (not just visible signs) and our intelligent use of the mind to grasp its meaning. In this way we shall bear fruit – some more, some less, but God is equally pleased with the hundredfold, sixtyfold and thirtyfold – he is looking for us to fulfil our potential and for fruit-bearing growth in our lives.

The harvest (Matt. 13:24–30; Mk. 4:26–29)

Matthew tells the story of a man who sows good seed in his field, but then an enemy comes at night and sows weeds there too. Both the wheat and the weeds grow together in the field. The owner refuses to allow his servants to try and remove the weeds lest they damage the true seed. Only at the final harvest will they be separated. Then the weeds will be burnt and the wheat gathered into the master's barn.

The emphasis in this story is on our need to wait for the final harvest. The judgement of the kingdom will not be apparent until the final judgement day. Until then the true and the false grow together in the kingdom. How true that is of the church! Many long to weed out the unspiritual from the church and develop a single-minded church consisting only of like-minded spiritual men and women. This parable shatters that sort of dream. In rooting out the weeds we shall damage some of the true believers, for our handling of people is never totally sensitive and discerning. We may even think that some of the true stalks of wheat are just weeds! So be patient with the church of God!

Mark's equivalent story is somewhat different. His emphasis is that the kingdom of God is like seed which grows without human effort. We merely see the growth of the seed and enjoy the end result in the harvest. So often a true work of the kingdom flourishes quite apart from our endeavours. There is something sovereignly mysterious about the working of God. We love to try to analyse the causes – 'Was it because people prayed or because evangelism became a priority or because . . .? Actually it was entirely due to God himself! Let us enjoy his working and gather in the harvest as he prepares it for us.'

Mustard seed and leaven **(Matt. 13:31–33; Mk. 4:30–32; Lk. 13:18–21)**

The tiny mustard seed becomes a mighty shrub. The leaven causes the bread to rise and become a significant loaf. The kingdom seems small and unimportant, but it grows. Jesus started as a small baby, but grew (Lk. 2:52). The church too started very small and only among Jewish people, but became gradually a large international movement. Each of us individually starts in the kingdom with new birth, but must grow in Christ until we enter the glory of being perfectly like our Lord.

From these two parables we learn not only that the kingdom grows, but also that we must not despise what is tiny and apparently insignificant. We love to boast of big churches and meetings. We are tempted to judge on the basis of statistics. But God may surprise us by making a tiny bit of leaven influence the growth of the whole church. A minuscule seed may become the great tree.

It should also be noted how the birds of the air find shade beneath the branches of that tree. From early times it was understood that the birds here represent the nations of the earth. Later we shall again note how the kingdom of God is for all nations. The tree of the kingdom was not just to give shelter to Jewish birds, but to all peoples.

Treasure and pearl (Matt. 13:44–46)

A farmer finds treasure in a field. A merchant finds a priceless pearl. Both sell all they have in order to buy it. The kingdom of God is of such immense value that it is worth sacrificing everything we have in order to enjoy it. To be totally under God's gracious rule is the secret of all joy in life. Only with the Lord do our lives have their true value and worth. When we come to the Lord for his life-giving salvation we surrender all we have and all we are to his control. So it was that the early church's baptismal creed was 'Jesus is Lord'. Jesus becomes our boss in every detail of life.

Many people fear the cost of becoming a follower of Jesus. They realise they may have to give up a girl or boy friend. They wonder what it will mean for their professional career. Will he push them into missionary work or into some other form of ministry? Will they become religious cranks and lose all their friends? They need not be anxious. The glories of Jesus Christ are worth any sacrifice and God loves us so much that he does not want to spoil our lives. He will enrich them beyond compare.

Good and bad fish (Matt. 13:47–50)

Just as the wheat and tares grow together in the kingdom, so also now the fishing net gathers in fish of every kind, both good and bad. This little parable again stresses the final judgement when God will 'separate the evil from the righteous, and throw them into the furnace of fire' (Matt. 13:49). It is not popular today to preach about heaven and hell. We prefer to talk about the blessings of the Christian life here on earth. But the New Testament has much to say about our ultimate future. It not only gives us the promise of an assured hope if we are true followers of Jesus Christ, but it also warns of 'the furnace of fire' where 'men will weep and gnash their teeth' (Matt. 13:50). It is good for us to be reminded of the final judgement which is the climax of the kingdom. The glories of eternal life with our beloved Jesus Christ encourage us to persevere even through hard times. The threat of damnation warns us not to play games with the living God. It alerts us too to the urgent need to share the good news of salvation in Christ with men and women all over the world.

Summary

So we see that the term 'kingdom' is rich and wide in its significance, covering many facets of God's gracious working in the world and for his people.

'The kingdom of God implies the whole of the preaching of Jesus Christ and his apostles,' says one commentator; another defines the kingdom of God as 'the basic theme which Jesus proclaimed, the core or essence of his teaching'; some rabbis described the kingdom of God as the very truth or essence of the law. The idea of the kingdom is virtually equivalent to the whole gospel. It has been said that the words 'kingdom', 'salvation' and 'eternal life' are almost interchangeable. In submission to God as king we find salvation and the assurance of eternal life. Certainly Matthew refers frequently to the gospel of the kingdom as the basis of the preached message (Matt. 4:23; 9:35; 10:7; 13:19; 24:14) and in Acts too Jesus and the apostles preach the kingdom of God (Acts 1:3; 8:12; 19:8; 20:25; 28:23, 31). Preaching Jesus, preaching the gospel and preaching the kingdom are just different ways of saying the same thing.

To remain truly biblical we must resist the temptation to narrow down the meaning or application of the kingdom of God to fit the particular bees in our bonnets. Each of us has our own particular bias, but we must not twist the scriptures to fit our interests.

All of us need the full-orbed teaching on the kingdom of God to correct our narrow vision and imbalance, to give us aspects of God's life-giving grace which we might otherwise lack.

2

It's God's Kingdom

Earthly kingdoms have clearly defined borders and can be marked out on a map. It is also clear which people belong as citizens. The kingdom of God is not like that. It does not have a geographical location and no particular group of people can claim it as theirs. God's sovereign rule stands above all humanly defined limitations. God's ways are higher than ours and his working breaks out of the neat boxes into which we try to fit him.

Those of us who travel widely see something of this. God's Spirit is moving in significant ways in many different denominations around the world. In many parts of Latin America the big development of the church is through the Pentecostals, although Baptists and others play their smaller role. In West Africa it is often through churches founded by interdenominational missions that the Holy Spirit works most freely. In East Africa we see the Lord mightily at work through the Anglican church. In Indonesia and Korea God's kingdom is extended most of all through traditional reformed Presbyterian churches. In South Africa and Singapore charismatic churches have brought new life to many.

The kingdom of God is not bound by our narrow ideas of how the Holy Spirit should function. We may like to dictate to God how he should work, but the Bible stresses that it is *God's* kingdom, not ours. 'The Lord reigns' (Ps. 93:1) – not us!

Political powers

Nor do political powers or even Satan himself hold the trump card. The Old Testament constantly reiterates the fact that the Lord alone is king; there is no other king. He will not tolerate rivals to his kingship, for he is a jealous God whose glory shall not be taken by another. And Paul assures us in 1 Corinthians 15:24 that ultimately every rival 'rule and every authority and power' will be destroyed.

One of the great titles of God is that he is King of kings. He is Lord over all human kingdoms and rulers. In Daniel 2 the prophet presents the great king Nebuchadnezzar with his dream and its interpretation, showing how God has given Nebuchadnezzar all the power, might and glory he enjoyed. It is by the will of the great King of kings that Nebuchadnezzar has become a lesser king of kings, to whom 'the God of heaven has given the kingdom' (Dan. 2:37). Then Daniel shows the king how his empire will be followed by a succession of lesser empires until the advent of the messianic kingdom 'which shall never be destroyed' (2:44). The King of kings rules over history and determines the course of earthly kingdoms. The book of Revelation also gives a prophetic sweep of history, showing that finally the Lamb will conquer the kings of this world, because the Lamb is 'Lord of lords and King of kings' (Rev. 17:14).

Even today it is easy for us to forget that political powers do not have supreme control. The great nations and their leaders strut across the stage of history as if there were no God over them. But the truth remains that the kingdom of God rules sovereignly over the kingdoms of this world.

The devil

The great usurper of God's kingly rule is Satan himself. Although in truth he is still under God's kingly rule, he has snatched for himself quite considerable power as the 'ruler of this world' (Jn. 12:31; 14:30; 16:11; Eph. 2:2). Sadly he is indeed ruler over this world and over the multitudes of people who do not acknowledge Jesus Christ as their lord and king. God, however, does not allow even Satan to usurp his position as supreme king. When Jesus began his ministry he was immediately locked in battle with Satanic forces. He cast out demonic spirits, demonstrating his power over them, and he sent his disciples out to preach, heal and cast out demons. They rejoiced that the demons were subject to them in his name. Jesus then replied, 'I have given you authority . . . over all the power of the enemy' and he declared, 'I saw Satan fall like lightning from heaven' (Lk. 10:17–20). The culminating victory over the kingdom of the devil came through the death and resurrection of the incarnate Jesus. The prince of this world has been put down by the King of kings. The defeat of Satan will be finally completed in the great judgement. Meanwhile we rejoice that God is king over all demonic forces. We can defeat Satan now through the death of Jesus, by the word of our testimony and by our willingness to lay down our lives for the Lord (Rev. 12:11).

Miracles

The significance of the miracles Jesus performed – when he stilled the storm, healed the sick, cast out demons and raised the dead – was to demonstrate that 'the kingdom of God is at hand'. God's authoritative rule has come. His power has erupted into our midst. As Jesus says, 'if it is by the Spirit of God that I cast out demons, then the kingdom of God has come upon you' (Matt. 12:28). When he sends his twelve disciples out to preach that the kingdom of heaven is at hand, he also commands them to heal, raise the dead and cast out demons. Once too in the book of Acts the preaching of the kingdom is linked to signs and great miracles being performed (Acts 8:12–13).

When the powerful kingdom of God is present, we may expect things to happen! We shall not be surprised that miracles take place. They are given in order to show that the Lord is king indeed and that no other power can rival him. But Jesus also warns us not to overemphasise signs and wonders, for we

It's God's Kingdom

may easily be misled. False prophets may also show great signs and wonders, so that even God's chosen followers may perhaps be led astray (Matt. 24:24). All religions have their miracle-workers. Healings and apparent exorcisms are the normal stock-in-trade of special men or women in Islam, Hinduism, Buddhism, Judaism and all other faiths. Our God is characterised by humility, so he does not go in for sensationalism. Jesus even says that 'the kingdom of God is not coming with signs to be observed' (Lk. 17:20), but it is seen in the inner working of God which transforms our lives.

Christians in the West today are so insecure about the very existence of God that we reach out hungrily for evidence of his powerful working. We devour stories of sensational miracles overseas and sadly there are some Christians who delight to write what we long to read.

Recently I read a report from Malaysia in a Christian magazine. I have worked in this country and have many friends there, so I was interested in what it had to say. My suspicions were raised by the very tone of the article. Truth was twisted to prove certain prejudices – the writer definitely had one or two axes to grind! And it was sensationalist. I therefore gave the article to several Christian leaders from Malaysia to ask them their opinion. All were agreed that the so-called miracles were largely fabricated and untrue. Even basic facts were unreliable.

It is true that our God demonstrates the reality of his unique kingdom by defeating Satan the usurper. Gracious miracles of power are an integral part of his kingdom. We may expect exorcism and other evidences that he alone is king. But let us not be gullible, swallowing every exciting story! Let us use the spiritual gift of discernment!

Church leaders

Political powers and Satan himself are not the only ones who may take God's glory to themselves. Church leaders too may be tempted to become authority figures. The biblical picture of leaders is that they are to be shepherds who should care for their sheep, give an example and lead the way. Shepherds are not authority figures. Ministers too are called to serve – that is the very meaning of the word 'minister' – not to rule over their people. Jesus makes this very clear in Mark 10:42–45. In the political world of the Gentiles, he says, their leaders 'exercise authority', but he then firmly rejects that for his followers – 'it shall not be so among you'. Like slaves Christian leaders should serve in humility. Like Jesus himself they are to give their lives for others, not try to rule with authority.

It is so easy to allow church leaders to take over the place of God in our lives. As Christians we are all a 'royal priesthood' (1 Pet. 2:9), all in God's kingdom and all priests with direct access to God himself. Of course we have much to learn from our leaders as more experienced, mature and gifted believers, but they are not the necessary mediators of God's word to us.

The outworking of God's kingdom

'Thy kingdom come', we ask in the Lord's Prayer (Matt. 6:9–13). We long that God's rule should be evident here on earth. We want him to be king in fact, not just in theory. But what does it mean for God to be king? The context of the Lord's Prayer gives us the answer.

'Hallowed be thy name . . .'

The coming of God's kingdom is linked inseparably to the honour of his name. In the Old Testament the purpose of Israel's national life was that the name of their God should be glorified both by Israel herself and also by the surrounding Gentile nations. In the New Testament too this is the goal of the church. We are to worship the Lord. Our lives should reflect his character so that other people will see God's holiness and glorify him. We live to bring him honour. We long that people of all nations everywhere might recognise his perfection and give him the honour that is his due.

In his diaries Christopher Columbus delights in his name 'Christopher'. It derives from the Latin and means someone who bears Christ. Columbus felt that in his journeys to the Americas he was taking Christ to the unevangelised peoples there. Whatever we may feel about his practice, his ideals were in this respect right.

Missionaries in remote tribal areas often talk of village children coming out to welcome the visiting missionary with cries of 'Jesus is coming; Jesus is coming.' We smile at the naiveté which thinks that the missionary is Jesus himself. But actually the children are right. As Christians we carry Christ within us. When we come, Christ comes. What a responsibility! Through us the name of the Lord is to be hallowed. When people see us, how much do they observe of the love, holiness, humility and perfection of our king?

I would not like it if people made rude remarks about my wife or children whom I love. I delight to hear appreciative comments about them. Likewise we hate to see the name of the Lord dragged in the mud and long for it to be properly honoured.

'Thy will be done . . .'

The coming of God's kingdom involves us in obedience to his will. Jesus said, 'If you love me, you will keep my commandments' (Jn. 14:15). What is the will of God? The answer is clear: 'this is the will of God, your sanctification' (1 Thess. 4:3). Paul goes on to say that 'whoever disregards this, disregards not man but God, who gives his Holy Spirit to you' (1 Thess. 4:8). God's will is that we should be holy, and that is why he has given us his Spirit. The very name of the Spirit is highly significant – he is the *Holy* Spirit. God enjoys our praise and worship; he rejoices when we open our mouths to share the gospel in witness to our friends; he encourages us to have faith that he will work all sorts of miracles; he loves to open his ears to our prayers. But all those things pale into insignificance when compared with God's great desire for us that we should be holy, righteous and pure.

This then is the primary will of God. But how can we discover the details of God's commandments to us? It is no use talking about obedience unless we know what he asks us to do. God may speak to us in many ways, but the key is found in the study of his word, the Bible. As we soak ourselves in the scriptures, we shall grow in our understanding of the mind of Christ. We shall know him better and so also sense increasingly what he likes and what he does not like. God's revelation of himself has been preserved for us in the Bible so that we may know his will.

So when we talk about the kingdom, let us bear in mind its context of 'hallowed be thy name' and 'thy will be done'. The kingdom is for the honour of God rather than for our prosperity.

'The kingdom of our Lord and of his Christ' (Rev. 11:15)

The first three gospels give considerable emphasis to the kingdom, but in the epistles this changes. The kingdom is still mentioned from time to time, but now the writers are more interested in the central figure of the kingdom, Jesus himself, who is the Lord. Then in the final book of the New Testament, the book of Revelation, we are faced with the strange mixed metaphor of the royal lion of Judah who is the sacrificial Lamb of God (Rev. 5:5–6). And it is that Lamb who with God sits upon a throne (Rev. 22:1, 3).

What a strange picture! The king is no longer the proud lion, but the meek Lamb which has been slaughtered in sacrifice.

What do we learn from all of this?

Jesus the Lord is central

On the first day of a holiday houseparty in Switzerland we all took the boat along the beautiful lake. The water reflected the clear blue sky and the splendid mountains. It seemed almost out of place to get into deep conversation, but soon we all began to get to know each other. The man next to me was an elder in a traditional evangelical church.

'Is your church growing?' I asked. 'Are you getting new people joining the congregation and coming to know the Lord?'

'No,' he replied. 'People don't seem to want the gospel these days. But we have a fine minister who really preaches the word.'

After some further talk I formed the impression that my friend came from a church which had made its doctrine into an idol and therefore could not find the life and love of Jesus Christ.

In the kingdom of God Jesus Christ is central. Nothing else must take his place, however good and important it may be. Even sound biblical doctrine can become the pride and emphasis of the church, rather than Jesus himself. Of course we need a right biblical understanding of the Lord and his work for us, but the key to the kingdom rests in a living relationship with Jesus Christ.

We all find it easy to slip into error. We put excellent but lesser things at the centre of the stage. There are various idols which may take the pre-eminent place from Christ in our churches – sound doctrine, the gifts of the Spirit, our form of worship or music, church tradition, miracles of healing, loving fellowship, good biblical scholarship. All of these are good and some even vital, but none of them serves any useful purpose if Jesus is toppled from his supreme throne. *He* is the king of the kingdom.

Just before this Swiss houseparty I had been studying 1 Corinthians as I lay in a hospital bed. The centrality of Jesus had impressed me. Wisdom and power are excellent, Paul declares. God himself is both wise and powerfully strong. But power and wisdom are found supremely in Jesus Christ (1 Cor. 1:24), so let us not get stuck on lesser things. Let us boast only in the Lord himself (1 Cor. 1:31).

Then I began a study of Colossians and was excited to notice the same point. Again Paul underlines that 'all things were created through *him* and for *him*' (Col. 1:16) so that *Christ* might be pre-eminent in all things (Col. 1:18).

Suffering and the kingdom

The book of Revelation spoke to a persecuted church with the triumphant message that the forces of evil will be vanquished and that God will triumph. The writer picked up the expression 'Lamb of God' from John 1:29 and from the whole sacrificial system of the Old Testament. He showed that, like the persecuted church, Jesus too suffered in apparently weak meekness as the Lamb who is worshipped with God as the King of kings. The kingdom belongs not only to God but also to his Messiah (Rev. 11:15) and the righteous will be vindicated.

The Bible contains this amazing paradox. God comes to earth in the form of a servant. He lays aside his glory. He is born not in a palace, but in a stable. He is rejected, despised and finally crucified. He is taken down from the cross, a cold corpse laid to rest in a dank tomb. We know that in theory he has the power not only to lay down his life but also to take it up again. But he has purposely shed his power. The New Testament therefore carefully uses a passive tense for the resurrection – Jesus *was raised*; he did not raise himself. He was dead, but God raised him up (Acts 2:32).

The foremost title for Jesus in the minds of the early apostles was 'the suffering servant'. The king does not just reign in glorious power; he suffers and serves like a slave.

As Christians we must learn an unnatural lesson. If we want to reign with Christ and enjoy the resurrection life of his kingdom, then we must follow in his footsteps of suffering and humble slave-like service. The slave enjoys no rights. So it is written that if we suffer and endure, then we shall also reign with Christ (2 Tim. 2:12). Paul knew the reality of fellowship with Christ in suffering. He therefore understood the true purpose of divine power in the Christian life. He did not want to use power to escape from sickness and suffering, but rather to enable us to persevere in endurance and joyful patience in the midst of suffering (Col. 1:11).

'May you be strengthened with all power, according to his glorious might,' Paul wrote. I can imagine some modern Christians reading that verse from Colossians and stopping at that point. Yes, power is the name of the game today. We want our mighty God to demonstrate his superiority and his reality by miraculous deeds of power. And he does! In his grace he loves to show weak Christians that he really does exist and that he does work today. He is also a jealous God who hates occult spirits or other deities being thought to be more glorious than he is. So he shows by signs and wonders that he is above them all. But Paul is not talking about that sort of thing in this verse. We must allow him to finish his sentence: 'May you be strengthened with all power, according to his glorious might, *for all endurance and patience with joy . . .*' And what a miracle that is! In Christ we can be given the glorious power to suffer with patient, joyful endurance.

The throne of God is occupied by a suffering Lamb. Sacrifice is the door to the kingdom. When Jesus saw that John the Baptist was in prison facing martyrdom, then he began to preach that the kingdom was at hand (Matt. 4:12, 17). Twenty-eight times the book of Revelation calls Jesus 'the Lamb' to underline this vital truth that entry into and enjoyment of God's kingdom means suffering service.

Some who advocate political revolution in order to establish the kingdom of God may find the biblical Jesus too weak for their liking. Others who believe that kingdom life means success-orientated prosperity may actually reject the suffering servant lamb as too poor. Yet others who emphasise God's miracles of healing leave little room for the reality of suffering and death. But the Bible clearly shows our Lord as weak and poor and one who suffered deeply. 'A servant is not greater than his master' (Jn. 13:16). As members of God's kingdom we too must be prepared to follow this difficult path.

3

Entering the Kingdom

In the last chapter we saw that the kingdom belongs to God. Happily our God loves to give with generous grace, so he shares the kingdom with us. As Jesus said, 'it is your Father's good pleasure to give you the kingdom' (Lk. 12:32).

How do we enter the kingdom?

It is when the kingdom is preached that we can understand it, appreciate it and enter into it. As Paul points out, we cannot believe without hearing, and we cannot hear without the preached word (Rom. 10:14).

But words have lost their credibility today. Many of us prefer political action or visible signs of the working of God's Spirit rather than 'mere preaching'. Of course the word should be accompanied by the visible signs of God at work, not only in the miraculous but also in the holiness and fellowship of God's people. But the Bible constantly stresses the central importance of words. It was by his word that

God created the world and it was as the Word of God that Jesus came to serve us (Jn. 1). So we are not surprised to find that the New Testament talks much of the word or good news of the kingdom.

Repentance

When the reality of the kingdom comes near us, the first response should be repentance. We have already noted this emphasis in the preaching of the kingdom by John the Baptist and by Jesus himself. When we repent and God restores us to himself, he and all in heaven rejoice (Lk. 15:6, 10, 32).

What then is repentance? The Greek word signifies a complete about-turn of the mind, like a squad of soldiers turning round to march in the opposite direction. It should be noted firstly that it is the *mind* which changes direction, not just our actions. There is a constant emphasis in the Bible that our minds and our thinking direct the course of our lives.

Before we heard the message of the kingdom of God and his salvation we were under the control of Satan, whether we knew this consciously or not. He was the prince of our lives and he led us into sin and unbelief. Now we are to turn around and follow Jesus Christ as our supreme Lord and our guide. We shall come to hate the sin that spoilt our lives and stopped us giving God the honour due to him. Turning from Satan and sin, we now lovingly follow the Lord and obey him in holiness.

This repentance may well involve us in making restitution for the sin of the past. We may well have to confess to other people if we have in some way

Entering the Kingdom

harmed them. We shall certainly have to confess our sin and say 'sorry' to God himself.

In entering the kingdom of God we are making a clean break with sin and the rule of Satan. If we have had occult connections in the past through Ouija boards, spiritism, witchcraft, Eastern religious practices, astrology or anything else which may open the door to evil spirits, then we need to repent of this and definitely break any link with it. We may well need prayerful help from others in order to clean out the demonic influence of Satan.

Faith

Together with repentance comes the need for faith. Faith is not just an academic exercise in which we are mentally assured that the good news of Jesus is the truth. Faith implies a definite trust in Christ as our Lord and Saviour. To trust someone is much more significant than just believing in their existence! I believe in the existence of the devil, but I don't trust him!

Believing in Christ is like getting into a swimming pool. There are lots of other people already in the water enjoying a good swim. How do you enter the water and join them? Some people dive in without hesitation, find the cold a shock but quickly adjust and enjoy it. Others go quietly to the shallow end, gently but unhesitatingly going deeper and deeper into the water until they launch themselves into a good swim. I tend to hover near the edge, feel the water with my toes and put off the climactic decision to dive into the cold water. Everybody assures me that it is lovely in, but my toes tell me that others' assessment may not be quite true! Finally, however, I know that a decision has to be taken, and I jump in. Sadly there are also some people who reject the advice of those who are already in the water and they determine not to swim at all. They miss so much.

Belief in Christ involves a commitment to him which is irrevocable. Some people come to this commitment quickly, some slowly. Some enter the kingdom gradually, step by step, while others dive in suddenly and decisively. How we enter does not matter. The fact that we do enter is what is important.

The cross and the resurrection

Some while back I was interviewing a young applicant to All Nations. He told me warmly of his conversion experience and enthused about his new faith. He was obviously enjoying his new experience of fellowship and worship with others of like mind. But as he talked I became increasingly uneasy.

What was the basis of his conversion? Who or what did he believe in? Faith is good, but to enter the kingdom of God it needs to be faith in Jesus Christ, his atoning death and resurrection. I asked him in what way the death of Jesus had been important for his conversion. Surprisingly he did not feel it had been important at all. After considerable further questioning I ended up with the impression that his faith and conversion were just a heart-warming emotional experience.

To enter the kingdom we require faith in the historical person of Jesus the Messiah. It is through his sacrificial death on the cross that we can be born again. On the cross he has taken the penalty of all our sin, opening the door for total forgiveness and cleansing.

A while ago I was speaking at a Christian conference in Germany. At one stage I talked about the cross of Christ and the total cleansing we can obtain through his shed blood. A very respectable German businessman aged about sixty came to me at the end of the conference in tears. He had been involved in herding thousands of Jews into the gas chambers. Can the Christian's conscience ever be purified from such horrific sin? 'Yes,' I assured him. 'If we confess our sins, the blood of Jesus ... cleanses from *all* sin' (1 Jn. 1:9, 7).

Perhaps our memories are not darkened by such appalling evil, but many of us too find that certain misdemeanours in the past haunt us and we still feel unclean. It is good to be reminded that Christ's sacrificial death washes us totally.

Just as we are joined together with Christ in his death, so too we are raised with him to new life. God raised the cold corpse of Jesus from the grave — he lifts us up too from our past lives into the new resurrection life with Jesus Christ.

New birth

'Unless one is born anew, he cannot see the kingdom of God,' Jesus said to the godly Jewish leader Nicodemus (Jn. 3:3). We have to be transferred from the old life under Satan and sin before we can enter God's kingdom. Then we are raised to that new life in the resurrection. When we come to faith in Jesus Christ, we start a new spiritual life like a new-born baby starting its physical life.

We commonly translate John 3:3 as being 'born again', but actually the word used could mean 'born from above'. This experience is not only the start of a new life, it is also a birth which comes from above, from God himself. We cannot convert ourselves. This is the work of God in us and for us. We need the Lord to bring us into that new life where we can see God's kingdom and consciously come under his dominion.

Baptism and the Holy Spirit

The new birth is commonly linked to baptism and the gift of the Holy Spirit. In John 3 Jesus goes on to say that we cannot enter God's kingdom unless we are 'born of water and the Spirit' (Jn. 3:5). Water may here refer to baptism, but it could also be a delicate way of saying that we should not only be born as a result of sexual intercourse but also by the Spirit.

Baptism is the outward mark of belonging to God's people in the community of God's kingdom. It is the sign of the salvation God has promised to give all who believe in Jesus Christ. Repentance, faith, new birth and baptism go hand in hand. Then we need to add to that list the gift of the Holy Spirit. When we are born again, Jesus comes to live in us by his Spirit. Being born again includes receiving the Holy Spirit. Then as we grow in our new life we need to be constantly filled with the Spirit, so that he can make us increasingly like Christ in holiness, giving us all the fruit of the Spirit. He will also give to us those spiritual gifts which will be of benefit to the church and to ourselves. He will equip us for whatever ministries he calls us to.

How then do we enter the kingdom? By repentance and faith in the cross and resurrection of Jesus, by new birth from above, baptism and the Holy Spirit. So God redeems us and gives us eternal life through the forgiveness of our sin.

Conditions of entry

The outsider

Who can enter the kingdom? 'The pious, not ordinary people of the land – men, not women – Jews, not Gentiles.' This was the thinking of some at the time of Jesus. Jesus shatters such élitism by revealing himself more clearly to the woman of Samaria (Jn. 4:1–42) than to anyone else throughout his ministry on earth. She was certainly no model of pious decorum! And John 4 underlines the word 'woman' again and again to emphasise that Jesus was breaking through the male chauvinism of current religion. Even his disciples 'marvelled that he was talking with a woman' (Jn. 4:27)! And she was a Samaritan, not a Jew – 'Jews have no dealings with Samaritans' (Jn. 4:9).

As Donald Kraybill points out in his book *The Upside-Down Kingdom*, it is the poor, the outcast, the despised who are welcomed into the kingdom. The king invites to his feast the tramps who sleep by the roadside. The despised sinners and tax-collectors become his disciples. The rejects of respectable society are welcomed. Indeed it is shown to be much more difficult for the rich, the respectable and the powerful to enter the kingdom (Mk. 10:17–27).

The Pentecostal churches of Latin America illustrate this truth. Why do they grow so rapidly among the poor in the shanty towns? It is partly because these so-called dregs of society are thrilled to find that God esteems them. Being so poor, they cannot afford doctors, so services of healing attract them. The despised shanty-town people feel they are somebody in the church. Everyone calls them 'brother' or 'sister'; their testimony is greeted with cries of 'glory to God'. They can participate in the worship and be listened to with respect. And as they grow in Christian experience, they are given responsibility in church ministries. In the church and in the kingdom we all become people of significance. As Kraybill beautifully points out, in the kingdom 'everyone is the greatest'. Francis Schaeffer has said likewise that there are no 'little people' in the kingdom; all have the same status as God's children and heirs. The kingdom knows no hierarchy.

Humility

As we have seen, in Mark 10:17–27 Jesus teaches with shattering clarity how hard it is for the rich to enter the kingdom of God. Immediately before, people had brought children to Jesus (Mk. 10:13–16). He was in the middle of teaching his disciples and the children disturbed the peace. 'Don't bring the children in here! Get them out!' the disciples snapped. But Jesus was angry and said, 'Let the children come to me . . . for to such belongs the kingdom of God' (Mk. 10:14). If they belong to the kingdom, they can come to the king. To enter the kingdom we must become like little children – powerless and small. The Lord declares, 'this is the man to whom I will look, he that is humble and contrite in spirit, and trembles at my word' (Isa. 66:2). Was this word in Jesus' mind when he taught: 'Blessed are the poor in spirit, for theirs is the kingdom of heaven' (Matt. 5:3)?

Some years ago I did a Bible study on meekness and humility. I was challenged when this revealed that virtually all God's blessings and gifts are at some stage in scripture associated with meekness. Adult pride must give way to childlike meekness if we are to enter the kingdom. Vanity and self-assertiveness have no place under God's rule.

The cost

The Christian claims: 'Jesus is our king. We will do anything for him. We will go anywhere he wants us to serve him.'

The gospels call such self-sacrificing discipleship for the sake of Christ 'taking up our cross'. We are to nail our own desires and ambitions to the cross of Jesus so that we can then follow him in total slave-like obedience. Jewish rabbis called this total submission 'the yoke of the kingdom', so Jesus will have associated kingdom life with absolute obedience to God's law. He himself gave us the perfect example of this. In the Garden of Gethsemane he won through to the position where he could say to his heavenly Father 'not my will, but thine, be done' (Lk. 22:42). Happily we can rest assured that God's will is not that of an evil tyrant, but is 'good and acceptable and perfect' (Rom. 12:2). Such death to our own desires and natural selves leads to the new life of the resurrection in Christ. When we die in that way, the Holy Spirit of Christ can fill us and renew us. And that is far better than anything the world can offer!

'So therefore, whoever . . . does not renounce all that he has cannot be my disciple' (Lk. 14:33). Discipleship in the kingdom is radical. We need to count the cost before we enter God's kingdom and submit to his kingship. We shall be following a Lord who suffered. 'Foxes have holes, and birds of the air have nests; but the Son of man has nowhere to lay his head' (Lk. 9:58). Jesus goes on then to say, 'No one who puts his hand to the plough and looks back is fit for the kingdom of God' (Lk. 9:62). To such obedient believers he offers the new life of the kingdom, a joyful relationship with God the Father through Jesus Christ, and the fruit and ministry of the Spirit. This is the gift of eternal life.

Pass it on!

'Fellow workers for the kingdom of God' (Col. 4:11) – that is what God is looking for. Disciples of Christ are not only to enjoy the life of the kingdom for themselves, but also to work together with other

Entering the Kingdom

believers in promoting God's kingdom in the world.

This is not a fun game; it will be hard work which will surely require disciplined obedience to Christ's word. Our work is *'for* the kingdom of God' and should lead to God's dominion being extended, so that new subjects are constantly being added to his kingdom. Such 'evangelism' or 'witness' longs for God's honour in the world and therefore that his rule should be acknowledged. Of course we also desire that other people should gain the salvation and rich blessings of the kingdom, but that is not our primary motive. We are called to be fellow-workers *for the kingdom of God*, that God may be king over all.

4

Kingdom Life

A number of years ago I was due to speak at a university Christian Union. I felt happy with the biblical exposition they had asked me to give as the message for that evening. Travel directions and questions of hospitality were all in order. But what about my appearance? The old days when speakers wore neat dark suits were definitely gone. Casual, informal gear seemed the thing. At that stage men students were into shoulder-length hair, but I was too old for that. A compromise seemed in order – not too short, but not right down to the shoulders.

The meeting went well and the students were enthusiastic. The Lord had spoken and brought blessing.

The next day I drove to a more traditional church for the weekend. I duly put on my dark blue suit and respectable tie. But what about my hair? My wife reminded me that Sunday lunch would be taken with two elderly prayer supporters. A conservative hair-style was required. My wife gave me a trim and I set off in the car.

Kingdom Life

'It's good to see you don't have long straggly hair like so many men these days,' one of the ladies greeted me. I shared with her the difficulty of being all things to all people unless one possessed a range of wigs for all styles of meeting. I assured her that to me the length of one's hair has no significance whatsoever. It is sad that little details of that nature can open or close people's ears to the word of God. I was reminded of Paul's word in Romans 14:17, 'the kingdom of God is not food and drink [nor hair-style or clothing] but righteousness and peace and joy in the Holy Spirit'.

The life of the kingdom has immeasurably rich characteristics. It seems a pity to give too much importance to trivial legalistic details. Paul himself was free to place himself under the restrictions of the law if that would help him win for Jesus Christ those who were under the law (I Cor. 9:19–23). But he was also happy to be free from the law for those who boasted of their freedom. How free are we? Are we happy to be old-fashioned and legalistic when that is appropriate, but also free and informal when that fits?

Above all, we should be positive! The kingdom, Paul says, is righteousness, peace and joy in the Holy Spirit (Rom. 14:17).

Righteousness

'When Messiah comes, he will bring in a kingdom of righteousness. When Israel is righteous even just for a moment, then the kingdom will come.' So the Jewish people have asserted for centuries, linking the coming of the kingdom of heaven with holy righteousness. And still today Jews question the Christian claim that the kingdom has come through the person of Jesus, because they note that holy righteousness has not yet been established.

Wonderfully the New Testament stresses that the coming of God's kingdom does not have to be earned by our righteousness, but is a gift of God's abounding and merciful grace. Although we are sinners and do not reach God's perfect standards of righteousness, yet Jesus takes our sin on to his own shoulders, bears that sin for us on the cross and then gives us his righteousness. Talking of Jesus Christ, Paul says that God 'made him to be sin who knew no sin, so that in him we might become the righteousness of God' (2 Cor. 5:21). So God covers us and our sin with the cloak of his own perfect righteousness. When God therefore looks at us, all he sees is Christ and his righteousness. Paul loves to say that we are 'in Christ' (e.g. Rom. 8:1). 'Blessed are those . . . whose sins are covered' (Ps. 32:1 quoted in Rom. 4:7). In Christ we are reckoned to be righteous despite our sin.

The traditional Jewish emphasis on kingdom righteousness is particularly clear in the apostle Paul's writings. While clearly teaching that we as sinners are reckoned to be righteous in God's eyes, Paul nevertheless stresses the absolute necessity of actual righteousness in daily living. The majority of his references to the kingdom relate to the question of holiness in everyday behaviour. He repeatedly warns that unholy people will not inherit or enter into God's kingdom and so he urges his readers to lead lives that are worthy of God (1 Cor. 6:9–10; Gal.

5:19–21; Eph. 5:5; 1 Thess. 2:10–12; 2 Thess. 1:5). The writer to the Hebrews likewise quotes from Psalm 45:6–7 to affirm, 'the righteous sceptre is the sceptre of thy kingdom. Thou hast loved righteousness and hated lawlessness' (Heb. 1:8–9). Matthew, the great writer on the kingdom, also underlines this connection between the kingdom and righteousness. The kingdom sermon, called the Sermon on the Mount, emphasises righteousness and exhorts us all to 'seek first his kingdom and his righteousness' (Matt. 6:33).

The Jews have traditionally taught that the kingdom will come only when Israel demonstrates true righteousness. While the New Testament continues that emphasis on righteousness, it is aware that actually all of us fail and sin sneaks into all our lives all the time. Therefore the coming of God's kingdom through Jesus Christ rebukes us for our sin and calls us to repentance. If we are to be people of the kingdom here on earth we must be marked by holiness of living. And if we are to inherit the fullness of the kingdom in the glory of eternal life, then we must demonstrate righteousness. This is the work of the Holy Spirit in us. He it is who can change us into the very likeness of Christ and transform us into holy people.

Justice

An oppressive regime suppressed the demands of the people. The occupying army served the interests of the foreign imperialist power. Human rights were trampled into the dust. Religious sensitivities were flouted. The Jewish people in this context remembered all the prophetic promises of a national deliverer. Messianic expectations ran high. Various charismatic figures had gathered crowds around them and begun rebellions against the Romans, only to be mercilessly crushed. Was Jesus of Nazareth the true Messiah? Would he be the new king like David of old who had led Israel into its heyday of national prosperity and power? Would Jesus be the king to defeat the Romans and deliver Israel? Rumours of a political messianic king ran through the Jewish crowds like wildfire.

What a disappointment! Jesus firmly denied that he was that sort of king. He didn't go in for violent revolution. His disciples and he remained unarmed. When the crowds wanted to make him their king, he slipped away from them to avoid such prominence. He even said, 'My kingship is not of this world; if my kingship were of this world, my servants would fight' (Jn. 18:36). And his triumphal entry into Jerusalem was not on a war-horse, but riding on a donkey. Jesus is the meek servant king, not the powerful political figure people hoped for.

But the life and message of Jesus does have socio-political significance. At the outset of his ministry he applied to himself the words of Isaiah 61 that he was to preach good news to the poor, release to captives, recovery of sight to the blind, liberty for the oppressed (Lk. 4:18–19). His message so disturbed the status quo that both religious and political authorities were threatened and crucified him as 'king of the Jews'. As Schechter points out,[1]

---

[1] Schechter, *Aspects of Rabbinic Theology*, p. 106.

'bad government is incompatible with the kingdom of God'. Why is that?

In the Old Testament righteousness and justice are linked together like Siamese twins. They must not be separated. Justice *is* righteousness expressed in society. Personal and individual righteousness should go hand in hand with a deep concern for social righteousness. Traditionally in Jewish thought on the kingdom of heaven, righteousness and justice together were to characterise the life of the kingdom. It is of course vitally important that each of us develops a true purity of life and we all know the scandal caused by financial, sexual or other forms of sin. But God is equally concerned about our social relationships in society, at work, in our community, at home. In fact Paul's injunction to be filled with the Spirit leads on to a long section about our social relationships (Eph. 5:18–6:9). And it is in the context of these social relationships that he gives his famous teaching about our need to put on the whole armour of God (Eph. 6:10–20). God hates it when his children engage in warm worship and lead morally upright lives, but oppress their employees at work or indulge in élitist attitudes to people of other racial backgrounds.

Feed the hungry, give water to the thirsty, clothe the naked, visit the sick and those in prison. So Jesus urged his followers. Then the king will say: 'Come, O blessed of my Father, inherit the kingdom prepared for you' (Matt. 25:34–36).

The Christian is called to help the needy and alleviate the sufferings of those who are poor and oppressed. It is deeply distressing to see the fearful injustices between the 'haves' and the 'have-nots', particularly in our cities and in developing countries around the world. God himself sides with such marginalised people. Jesus showed particular concern for despised publicans and sinners, children, women, Gentiles, harlots. Kraybill called his book *The Upside-Down Kingdom*: the kingdom of God is not for the rich and powerful so much as for the poor and despised.

But such social concern may sometimes prove inadequate. We may need to deal with the political causes of social sufferings. Let me give an example.

A missionary couple in Latin America felt a deep compassion for the girls who came into the big cities from their country background. The missionaries broke their hearts as they saw these simple girls being trapped by rich and powerful men who ensnared them in prostitution rackets. The missionaries began to befriend some of these girls, bringing them into the fellowship of the church and opening the door to a new life. Some of the girls began to leave the brothels, encouraged and helped by the Christian community. Then two men visited the missionaries. 'If you don't leave our girls alone, you will be in trouble,' they threatened. The men warned them that civic, military and police leaders were actually running these prostitution rackets. If the missionaries were roughed up, their children molested and their homes destroyed, it would be no use expecting justice from the authorities! What should they do?

Evangelistic witness and social concern soon got those missionaries into political issues up to their necks. This would have been equally true had they tried to help poor peasants suffering at the hands of greedy landlords and the grave inequalities of land ownership. It is no use Christians claiming to be apolitical. Justice may demand political involvement.

While in the Old Testament the twin words 'righteousness' and 'justice' occur together with great frequency, in the New Testament the idea of justice is clearly present but the word is missing. I would like to suggest that the word 'fellowship' takes its place. In the Old Testament justice was to be practised primarily in the community of God's people Israel; in the New Testament fellowship is also within God's people, the church.

What is fellowship? A cup of coffee together? Prayer and praise together? Well, it may include both of those, but fellowship is much deeper than that. The kingdom life means such richly loving community life that we are willing to share even our material possessions for the good of all. The early church so loved each other that they voluntarily shared their goods (Acts 2:44–45; 4:32) – the word used by Luke for 'in common' has the same root as the word for 'fellowship'. Kingdom life breaks down all the barriers of colour, wealth and status. Love motivates us to remove any hindrance to such fellowship by the appropriate sharing of all we have and all we are. Justice is to be practised in loving fellowship in the Christian community. The kingdom life is not individualistic, but involves us in the community of God's people. And God's people are not just to enjoy selfishly the rich privilege of belonging to God in his kingdom, we are to serve the wider community in society. Righteousness and justice / fellowship will be seen primarily within God's church, but we are to work and preach to spread it in the world.

Peace

'Seal your love with a kiss,' the minister said to a young couple at a wedding I was attending. A kiss is the outward sign of union together. 'Righteousness and peace will kiss each other', the psalmist wrote (Ps. 85:10). Paul confirms this in Romans 5:1, where he affirms that we have peace with God because we are reckoned to be righteous through our faith in Jesus Christ. Isaiah too saw that in the messianic kingdom peace, righteousness and justice would go together – 'Of the increase of his government and of peace there will be no end, upon the throne of David and over his kingdom . . . with justice and with righteousness' (Isa. 9:7).

Peace with God

Thanks to the sacrificial death of Jesus on our behalf, God becomes our father and friend. The holy judge has become the loving Father. We have been reconciled with God and can now live in a relationship of peace with him.

Because of bad experiences with their earthly father many people find it hard to enjoy that peace which Jesus has won for us. They always feel that God is distant, uncaring or unduly demanding. As a result they may fear God and serve him without a right enjoyment of peace. If this is true of you, share it with another Christian and allow them to pray with you and love you. Take time to meditate on your heavenly Father's unchanging and unconditional grace and love.

Peace in the church

Two women in the church did not agree with each other and they quarrelled. A typical church scenario? It may be, but Paul was so worried about it that he wrote to the Philippian church and urged the two women to make it up (Phil. 4:2–3). He realised that it would help if others in the church encouraged and assisted them towards reconciliation. And he showed them all the basis for peaceful relationships – the humble self-sacrificing example of Jesus. We are to be like Jesus in doing nothing out of selfishness or pride. Then we will find it easier to be loving and of one mind (Phil. 2:1–8).

'It is beautiful how Jewish and German Christians can be reconciled and can love one another as Christians,' I observed to a Jewish Christian who shared the platform with me in a meeting. He smiled ruefully. 'I wish I could win through to actually loving Germans. Many of my family perished in the gas chambers and I still cannot forgive the German people, even German Christians.' How well one understands, but failure to forgive will blight Christian growth.

The heart of the Christian message lies in God's forgiveness, reconciliation, peace and love. Our lives deny these fundamental truths if we do not live in loving peace with our brothers and sisters in Christ. But what joy it is to experience the living reality of Christian fellowship and community.

Peace with our neighbour

'So far as it depends on you, live peaceably with all' (Rom. 12:18). People may dislike, criticise or do bad things to us, but the Christian should not reciprocate and return evil for evil.

I was staying with someone recently whose next-door neighbour had had some bad experience of Christians as a young person. Now he was furious that his neighbours were Christian. He refused ever to greet them or speak to them. They tried every possible sign of friendliness, but he snubbed them. Then he began damaging their garden fence and knocking down their flowers. What should they do? In theory the answer was simple – be patient, go on loving, from their side having an attitude of peace towards him. I also joined them in prayer that their neighbour would either move house or come to a transforming faith in Jesus Christ – preferably the latter!

Peace within ourselves

Books on pastoral counselling abound today with their insightful teaching on the development of our personality. We need this. We live in a rat-race society with its fast-changing culture, unstable or broken marriages, no security of employment, depersonalised relationships at work and in society.

This all leaves its mark on us. Many today feel such personal insecurity and lack of self-value that it is hard to enjoy the serenity of inner peace. Some may be helped by prayer ministry, others by pastoral counselling; all will need the supportive love of fellow Christians and encouragement to meditate on the abiding love and grace of Jesus Christ.

Joy in the Holy Spirit

The third characteristic of kingdom life listed by Paul in Romans 14:17 is joy in the Spirit. Jesus told his disciples that they should particularly rejoice because their names were written in heaven (Lk. 10:20). The assurance of eternal life gives us even greater joy than seeing demons cast out or other miraculous signs of God in action, Jesus tells them.

In the kingdom we have the joy of being adopted as God's children and heirs. We not only rejoice to have God as our loving Father, but we also inherit all the riches of his grace. In the life of the kingdom he delights to fill us with his Spirit, who will graciously give us his fruit of holy living (Gal. 5:22–23) and those gifts which will enable us to play our part in the edification of his church.

It is sad when Christians are known as people with long faces. The New Testament constantly encourages us to be full of thanksgiving and rejoicing. As Christians we have so much for which to thank the Lord and so much to rejoice in. In Jesus' kingdom sermon, on the mountainside, the word for 'blessed' actually means 'happy'. 'Happy are the poor in spirit; happy are those who mourn; happy are the meek' (Matt. 5:3–11). This does not mean a glib, 'Smile, Jesus loves you,' which can be very forced and superficial. But the kingdom life imparts a deep-seated contentment and joy even in the midst of bereavement or other suffering. The Spirit makes us into people of joy.

This joy should also be shown in our worship. Even in times of deep repentance and confession or in times of quiet meditation our worship should be characterised by that same deep contentment in Christ.

Praise and worship form an integral part of life in God's kingdom. As the old rabbis have said, 'If there be no peoples praising him, where is the glory of the king?' Some of the great psalms of worship are known as the kingdom psalms (e.g Ps. 2; 18; 20; 45; 72). They were composed to express the joyful worship of God's people. From early times the Spirit has led God's people into worship through singing. Paul too talks of singing 'psalms and hymns and spiritual songs with thankfulness in your hearts to God' (Col. 3:16) – is it significant for us today that such praise is expressed in psalms, hymns and spiritual songs?! Let us be free to utilise a rich variety of musical forms in our worship. Paul also stresses here that our singing is 'with thankfulness' and it is 'to God', not just a good musical experience for our own satisfaction.

Power, not empty talk (1 Cor. 4:20)

The Jews had such reverence for the name of God that they hesitated to utter that sacred word,

Kingdom Life

preferring to use some other synonym. One such was 'power'—so Jesus talked of himself sitting at 'the right hand of Power' (Mk. 14:62). God was known as a God of dynamic power. He is not some cool deity sitting in the clouds impotently observing the world from on high. He is the God who by his word created the world and since then has been passionately concerned and active in the affairs of humankind. So it is not surprising that in the Lord's Prayer the kingdom, the power and the glory go together (Matt. 6:13, RSV footnote). Paul too knows that the kingdom comes in power, not in empty verbiage (1 Cor. 4:20) – the contrast is power versus empty words, not power versus words in general, for the context shows Paul using words to admonish and teach in the churches.

We expect our God to demonstrate his power. But how and to what effect?

At particular and significant times in history God has poured out evident signs of his power, but he has done so in markedly different ways. At the time of the exodus from Egypt God used Moses to show Pharaoh his miraculous power and to provide for the progress and daily needs of Israel. Then there was a remarkable outburst of miraculous signs in the time of Elijah and Elisha to underline the significance of their ministry in turning Israel away from the worship of Baal back to the true God. Both with Moses and with Elijah and Elisha God's power was shown through miracles.

The next climactic period of Israel's history was the age of the great prophets. In the space of just a few decades most of the Old Testament prophets lived and fulfilled their ministry. This time, however, God's power was not shown in sensational miracles, but rather through the power of his word. Still today we marvel at God's powerful word when we read Isaiah, Jeremiah and the other great prophets of that era.

After the great prophets Israel went through several centuries when God seemed to have withdrawn behind the clouds. What excitement then when the powerful words of John the Baptist captivated the crowds! And then Jesus the Messiah himself! The king and the kingdom had come. Again power was seen in Jesus' authoritative teaching and in the miracles he worked. People were amazed at his teaching and bowled over by his miracles – healing the sick, raising the dead, stilling the storm, casting out demons, producing money in a fish's mouth.

The early church followed in Jesus' footsteps. By the Holy Spirit their teaching and preaching produced powerful results. Their words were accompanied by miraculous signs. The gospels carefully link word and sign together. John's Gospel follows each miraculous sign with a chunk of Jesus' teaching. Matthew has long chapters filled with stories of Jesus' powerful works and then a long section of his teaching. Work and word must not be separated. In the Acts of the Apostles likewise the early Christians preach the gospel in power and demonstrate its reality by signs following.

Some Christians claim that after the first century miracles died out in the Christian church. This is historically untrue. It does seem to be true that in the Western church the emphasis was largely on preaching and teaching rather than on miracles of healing or exorcism. So God's power was demonstrated by great preaching. In the Eastern church, however, in Egypt and the Middle East, the desert fathers and monks continued to expect God's power to be shown through miracles of healing and exorcism as well as miracles of power over nature.

In the so-called Dark Ages a great struggle took place to win the pagan tribes of Europe to the faith of Jesus Christ. How did God's power manifest itself during this vital period of God's working in history? It was seen in the courageous, self-sacrificing faith of the intrepid Celtic missionaries. Although we might query some aspects of their doctrine, their deep spirituality and daring vision revealed the reality of God's sovereign reign.

Perhaps the next crucial period of church history was the Reformation. Again we do not see much evidence of sensational miracles, but we do see God's power at work, transforming not only individual lives but also the whole development of European religion and culture. God's power gave the Reformers an amazingly clear grasp of biblical essentials despite the prevailing religious corruption. When one reads Luther's or Calvin's commentaries, one is struck by their tremendous gift of biblical understanding and exegesis. These giant intellectual gifts were matched by self-sacrificing faith. Many of the Reformers died the death of a martyr. They were willing to pay the ultimate price to release God's power through the open Bible. And in fact God's word changed the whole course of

European history – that is surely God's power in action! And the Bible still retains its ability by the Spirit to change lives.

In the past century particularly we have seen God powerfully at work in the growth of his church throughout the world. The modern missionary movement has again demonstrated God's universal power. Sometimes healings and exorcisms have been an integral part of the missionary outreach, sometimes powerful preaching and teaching have been God's tool, sometimes the self-sacrificing lives of humble, loving Christian workers have been the proof of God's grace and power.

In Britain today we are seeing much more miraculous working than in previous times. In my own life too God's miraculous working in answer to prayer has played a significant role. There are exciting reports of remarkable miracles in much of Latin America and in China. But for some reason this does not seem generally to be the case in the Soviet Union or Afghanistan, despite the fearful persecution and material deprivation of oppressed Christians.

Miracles have no importance in themselves. They are merely one possible evidence or sign of God's kingdom at work. God is supremely concerned for the faith and holiness of his church and people. If miracles will help us believe with true holiness, then he may well give us such signs. If other demonstrations of the power of the kingdom suit us better, he fits his working to our needs. He is a God of loving grace.

When God does graciously give us miracles of healing, we need to remember that the kingdom is not yet perfectly present. There is still a future dimension to the kingdom, as we shall see in our next chapter. We are not therefore surprised when sickness and death are not totally overcome in this world. God knows when we need sickness to help us grow in faith and holiness, patience and hope. In a fallen world sickness and death are still a necessary part of our experience in life, but God gives grace to endure. Through suffering we may grow in our own character, in our relationship with the Lord and in our ability to counsel and help others in need. Sometimes he graciously heals us and delivers us from suffering, but sometimes he allows our sufferings to continue. This is the mystery of God's sovereignty and it is unwise for us to try to force God into our patterns. He is no genie of the lamp who will respond automatically to our faith and give us all we want. The Japanese theologian Kosuke Koyama has warned us of the danger of trying to 'domesticate God', making him into a domestic animal who does our bidding whenever we pray. God is king, not us!

We walk a tightrope. We may so stress miracles of healing that we face problems of faith when Christians are not healed or die. This is unreal and overemphasises the fact that the kingdom has already come without taking due note of the fact that the kingdom is not yet here in its fullness. Others of us may underemphasise God's miracle-working power and by our lack of faith quench the Spirit.

We believe in an all-powerful God. He can do all things. And we are his instruments if his Spirit is in us. He will demonstrate his sovereign kingly rule as he wills, to bring glory and honour to his name.

Universality

Right at the outset of his teaching ministry Jesus took the bull by the horns – God's grace was not just for Jews, but also for Gentiles of all races. The great prophet Elijah was sent to a Gentile woman in Sidon rather than to an Israelite widow. Elisha was used to bring healing to the Syrian Naaman, not to any of the lepers in Israel (Lk. 4:24–27).

Jesus surely knew that the best of Jewish tradition understood that the messianic kingdom would be for *all* peoples – and there has been a major strand of rabbinic teaching ever since which has stressed the universality of the kingdom. In the final messianic banquet people from all nations will share the feast together (Matt. 8:11).

In Matthew 14 Jesus fed a great crowd of some five thousand Jewish men plus an undisclosed number of women and children. No one queried his doing this. Even the Jewish authorities did not object to him feeding Jewish crowds. But in the following chapter we read of him miraculously feeding a further crowd of four thousand men. This was in a Gentile area and the indications are that it must have been a Gentile crowd. Feeding Gentiles – was this a sign of the messianic banquet? What right did Jesus have to do this? The Jewish leaders demanded proof from heaven (Matt. 16:1). Jesus replied with the enigmatic words that they would receive only the 'sign of Jonah' (Matt. 16:4). What did this mean? Was Jesus referring to Jonah's three days and nights inside the great fish and thus to his own death, burial and resurrection? Or was he referring to the fact that

Jonah was the only Old Testament prophet to be sent to preach to Gentiles in Nineveh?

The God of Israel is king in all the four corners of the world. The coming of his kingdom therefore requires that the gospel be preached to all nations – 'and then the end will come' (Matt. 24:14). In the fullness of the kingdom there must be people from every tribe, tongue, people and nation around God's heavenly throne to worship him (Rev. 5:9–14). We cannot experience the fullness of the kingdom life until we share in worship with people of all races, colours, ages and backgrounds.

This was the big issue in the New Testament church. Would the God of Israel accept Gentiles as followers of the Jewish Messiah without them joining the Jewish community and becoming like Jews? Is the Christian faith universal? Much of the New Testament deals with this question.[2] And it is still an issue today. Some Christians are so deeply involved in their own area of ministry that they have no interest in the rest of the world. Others even wonder whether people of other races and religions need Jesus Christ and the gospel. 'Are not other religions equally valid?' they ask. 'Arabs are Muslim, Indians are Hindu, Japanese are Buddhist, Jews

---

[2] For a fuller theological discussion of this, see J. Blauw's *The Missionary Nature of the Church* (Butterworth Press, 1962), R. de Riddler's *Discipling the Nations* (Baker Nook House, 1971) and the New Testament section of D. Senior and C. Stuhlmueller's *Biblical Foundations for Mission* (S.C.M., 1983). For a more popular overview, see my *What About Other Faiths* (Hodder, 1989).

are Judaists and Europeans used to be Christians.' The New Testament denies such ideas and shows Jesus Christ as the King of all peoples everywhere.

God's mercies in his kingdom are for both Jews and Gentiles (Rom. 11:11–32). It is in this context of God's mercies that Paul appeals to his readers to present their bodies as living sacrifices (Rom. 12:1). He does not ask us to give our spirits in God's service, but our bodies – Paul is so practical and down-to-earth! It's our bodies he wants! And probably our spirits will follow wherever our bodies go!

This, Paul says, is true spiritual worship (Rom. 12:1). Worship in the Spirit means self-sacrificing service in order that the mercies of God might reach out to Jews and Gentiles of all nations.

It is unbiblical to be narrow and insular in our attitudes. If we do not have a world-wide vision, we do not have the mind of Christ and we are missing a fundamental element in kingdom life. As George Beasley-Murray says in his major work on the kingdom of God, the nature of the kingdom is universality, righteousness and peace. These three form the heart of biblical teaching on the life of the kingdom. They should remain central in all we say, sing or think today about kingdom life.

5

It Has Come, It Will Come

Preaching in a strongly evangelical German church I was painting the exciting picture of God's plan for the future. I concluded by encouraging the Christians to pray, work and witness with that glorious goal in mind. Using Habakkuk 2:14 we noted the fact that the whole earth 'will be filled with the knowledge of the glory of the Lord, as the waters cover the sea'. When God's kingdom is complete, his glory will not be restricted to a few people hidden away in obscure corners. The whole earth will see his splendour in fullness. Every street in every town all over the world will be filled with the majestic presence of the living God.

The verse in Habakkuk related to Paul's parallel picture of 'the full number of the Gentiles' coming into God's kingdom and 'all Israel' being saved (Rom. 11:25–26). How we all must look forward to this great climax of history – those huge crowds of people from every nation and people, including multitudes of the Jewish race!

One of the church elders came to me after the service and thanked me warmly for my message.

'We must wait patiently and pray,' he said, 'for of course that glorious future day will only come when Jesus returns. Meanwhile we must just endure the godlessness of this age.'

My heart sank. My message had failed. Yes, I had excited people with the vision of the future, but somehow they had failed to see that we are already called now to be God's fellow-workers (1 Cor. 3:9; 2 Cor. 6:1) in moving towards the goal of God's perfect kingdom. It is of course true that we shall never achieve the perfection of God's kingdom life in this world, for that will indeed only come when Jesus returns in glory at his second coming. But meanwhile it is our happy task to move forward towards the fullness of life in the kingdom. Our evangelisation will extend God's rule increasingly. And then when the good news of the kingdom has been preached throughout the whole world to all nations, 'the end will come' (Matt. 24:14).

It is not only by world-wide evangelisation that we work towards the fullness of the kingdom. The apostle Peter says we are not only to wait for the kingdom, but also to hasten its coming (2 Pet. 3:12). But how does he say we can do that? His answer is straightforward: by 'lives of holiness and godliness' (2 Pet. 3:11). The perfect kingdom life will be seen in absolute holiness of life, both individually and in our relationships together. In the glory there will be no more sin. We shall experience unclouded love, the best that God can give us, the most 'excellent way' (1 Cor. 12:31). All other gifts will pass away, but complete trust in the Lord, assured hope which no longer experiences doubt, and the bliss of full love will go on and on for ever – this is eternal life. Such love for God and for other believers leaves no room for sin. We shall serve the Lord and worship him in perfect holiness and in complete harmony with all those who together with us are gathered around the throne of God.

Such a life of perfection in the kingdom requires a little practice now! It is the work of God's Holy Spirit to prepare us for eternal life.

Although the full perfection of kingdom life remains in the future, Jesus declared that it has already begun. This is the paradox of the biblical teaching on the kingdom. When Jesus the king came to earth two thousand years ago, he ushered in the kingdom. In the person of Jesus the kingdom has erupted into the world. And yet we await its full perfection and therefore pray 'thy kingdom come' in the Lord's Prayer. The Beatitudes in Matthew 5:3–12 reflect this paradox by using both present and future tenses – 'Blessed *are* . . . for they *shall* . . .'

Our knowledge of the future affects the way we live now, our aims in life and what we expect God to be doing in our midst. The perfect future gives us confidence even in difficult times now.

While it is true that we shall reign with Christ in the heavenly kingdom, we must not allow competitive pride to spoil our lives and relationships. This problem afflicted the first disciples of Jesus, and in our own different way we can fall into the same temptation. James and John betrayed their wrong attitudes through two requests. First: 'We want you to do for us whatever we ask of you' (Mk. 10:35). This demand shows they were looking rather for their own glory than for the glory of the Lord. But kingdom life is not selfish. It does not ask about the benefits we may get out of faith in Christ, but longs for Jesus Christ to be honoured.

The second request was equally disastrous! 'Grant us to sit, one at your right hand and one at your left, in your glory' (Mk. 10:37). As faithful disciples they expected and asked for the best positions in the kingdom. Surely they were better Christians than other people, they thought, so doubtless Jesus would be glad to honour them in this way. How easily selfish pride convinces us that we are superior to other believers! But they had a totally wrong idea of what Jesus' 'glory' actually meant. They thought of him on his kingdom throne in the splendour of the messianic banquet – and they wanted to share with him in that joy. But Jesus' glory is actually experienced in the suffering of his crucifixion, which Jesus calls 'my hour'. When he is about to be crucified he says, 'Now is the Son of man glorified' (Jn. 13:31). Who then would sit at Jesus' right and left in his glory? Two thieves! James and John had quite a wrong idea of kingdom life! As we wait and prepare for the fullness of the kingdom, our way will include suffering.

But gloriously there is a resurrection beyond the cross and peace beyond all present suffering. In God's perfect kingdom the Lord will be perfectly with us and we with him (Rev. 21:3). The consequence of this unclouded relationship of God with us is that 'he will wipe away every tear . . . death shall be no more neither shall there be mourning nor crying nor pain any more'. Satan will be totally removed from the scene, sin will be no more, all will be blissfully perfect. What a prospect to warm our hearts!

Revelation 21 links our full salvation in the kingdom with the tragic judgement of those whose sin reflects the nature of Satan (Rev. 21:8) – the cowardly, faithless, polluted, murderers, fornicators, sorcerers, idolaters and liars. Together with the devil, the false prophet and all those whose names are not in Christ's book of life (Rev. 20:10, 14) they will be judged and thrown into 'the lake of fire'.

We have been warned! It is not only God's wonderful love and grace which thrust us out into the world to bring people into Christ's sure salvation; it is also the fact that people need to be saved from such a fearful judgement.

And we too need to be ready for the coming of Jesus in glory and for the day of judgement. In chapter 1 we listed some of the 'kingdom parables', but we omitted one that is important in this context. 'The kingdom of heaven shall be compared to ten maidens' (Matt. 25:1). The story is well known (Matt. 25:1–12). Five of the young women kept their lamps trimmed and ready, so they could welcome the bridegroom when he came. The five foolish ones failed to take oil for their lamps in preparation – presumably they did not expect the bridegroom to come yet. Jesus' parable graphically declares that as a result 'the door was shut' and despite their desperate cries of 'Lord, lord' the bridegroom said 'I do not know you.'

The punch-line of the story is 'Watch therefore, for you know neither the day nor the hour' (Matt. 25:13). Jesus may come at any time, so be constantly ready. Ever since the days of Jesus on earth his followers have expected the imminent return of Christ. He actually said to his disciples 'there are some standing here who will not taste death before they see the kingdom of God' (Lk. 9:27).

There are various possible interpretations of this verse, but as a result of such sayings Jesus' followers expected him to return very soon. Each generation since then has also thought he would come back in their time. And we today must also be ready and eager for his return.

The climax

In chapter 2 we saw that 'It's God's kingdom'; and now again we must finish the book by underlining the whole purpose of the kingdom life. It is 'that God may be everything to every one' (1 Cor. 15:28). It is good to have talked about righteousness and holiness, justice, miraculous signs and other characteristics of our experience of God's reign. But these are just means to an end. The purpose of everything is that God himself may be king over all.

All three persons of the Trinity show wonderful self-effacing humility.

The Holy Spirit glorifies Jesus, not himself. As Jesus said when talking about the work of the Holy Spirit, 'he will take what is mine and declare it to you' (Jn. 16:14–15). Whenever the Holy Spirit is clearly at work, people talk very little about the Spirit, but rather glorify Jesus Christ and talk much about him.

It Has Come, It Will Come 149

Jesus comes to earth to reveal the Father and to open the way for us to relate with the Father. Just as the Spirit points away from himself in order to glorify the Son, so now the Son's ministry is to be the way to the Father and to glorify him.

In his final great prayer before the crucifixion Jesus not only prays that the Father will glorify him (Jn. 17:1, 5), but also talks confidently of the glory that the Father has given to him (Jn. 17:22, 24). So the Spirit glorifies the Son, whose ministry it is to glorify the Father. The Father then delights in giving glory to his Son, for even God the Father is amazingly humble.[1]

But the final act in the life of the kingdom is that the Son gives all the glory back to the Father (Jn. 17:1). When the end comes, Jesus 'delivers the kingdom to God the Father' and destroys all possible rivals to his supreme reign (1 Cor. 15:24). This destruction of all rivals to the kingdom of God began with the miracles of Jesus, when he cast out demonic powers, defeated Satan, won the victory over sin, healed sicknesses, conquered death and overcame the forces of nature. These acts were signs of the victory of the kingdom, that God might reign supreme.

The highest summit of kingdom life is that God the Father should be honoured, worshipped and glorified. As we aim for the glories of the kingdom life we shall echo the worship of heaven where 'they fell on their faces before the throne and worshipped

---

[1] For a fuller study of relationships within the Trinity as a model for Christians see the author's *Jesus and His Relationships* (Paternoster, 2000).

God, saying, "Amen! Blessing and glory and wisdom and thanksgiving and honour and power and might be to our God for ever and ever! Amen" ' (Rev. 7:11–12).

If this little book causes us to fall on our faces before God's throne to worship the Father, then it has played its part in the life of the kingdom.

Questions for Discussion

Chapter 1

1 What does God do for us as our king today?
2 In what way could we be in danger of replacing God's kingship and submitting to human substitutes?
3 List the main point of each of the kingdom parables. How do they apply to us today?

Chapter 2

1 How does the unique kingship of Christ relate to the role of our parents, the government and church leaders?
2 What 'idols' are you tempted to put above Jesus Christ?
3 Discuss the tension between faith in Christ as the all-powerful king and as the meek suffering servant. How does this work out in our Christian life?

Chapter 3

1. What does it mean to be 'born again'? How does Jesus' death on the cross make this possible?
2. Share with others your experience of the reality of new birth.
3. What 'cost' has there been for you in entering the kingdom? How has the Lord compensated you for these sacrifices?

Chapter 4

1. Repentance and righteousness – in practical terms what have these meant for you? How does this affect your life as a member of your church?
2. What are you doing and what could you do to bring greater social justice to your area or country or to the wider world?
3. Discuss the work of God's Spirit in bringing a) peace, b) joy, c) power.
4. What could you do to help in the spread of the gospel to all nations around the world?
5. Are non-Christian religions demonic? Or are they ways to God like Christianity? How do we as Christians view other religions?

Chapter 5

1. Do you tend to overemphasise the present reality of the kingdom?

Questions for Discussion

2 In what ways does our glorious future hope affect our lives today?
3 Are you 'watching' and ready for Christ's coming? If not, why not?
4 What aspects of our future glory thrill you most?

Bibliography

Easy reading

N. Anderson, *The Teaching of Jesus* (Hodder & Stoughton, 1983)

W. Chantry, *God's Righteous Kingdom* (Banner of Truth, 1980)

A. M. Hunter, *Christ and the Kingdom* (St Andrews Press, 1980)

D. Kraybill, *The Upside-Down Kingdom* (Marshalls, 1985)

M. Lawson, *The Unfolding Kingdom* (Kingsway, 1987)

H. Snyder, *Kingdom Lifestyle* (Marshalls, 1986)

J. Wimber, *Power Evangelism* (Hodder & Stoughton, 1985)

Harder Reading

M. Arias, *Announcing the Reign of God* (Fortress Press, 1984)

Bibliography

- G. R. Beasley-Murray, *Jesus and the Kingdom of God* (Paternoster Press/Wm B. Eerdmans, 1986)
- E. Castro, *Sent Free* (Wm B. Eerdmans, 1985)
- B. Chilton (ed.), *The Kingdom of God* (SPCK, 1984)
- G. E. Ladd, *The Gospel of the Kingdom* (Paternoster Press, 1959)
- G. E. Ladd, *The Presence of the Future* (SPCK, 1980)
- C. G. Montefiore and H. Loewe, *A Rabbinic Anthology* (Schocken Press, 1974)
- R. Padilla, *Mission Between the Times* (Wm B. Eerdmans, 1985)
- H. Ridderbos, *The Coming of the Kingdom* (Presbyterian & Reformed Publishing Co., 1962)
- S. Schechter, *Aspects of Rabbinic Theology* (Schocken Press, 1961)

Your Guide to Guidance

Martin and Elizabeth Goldsmith

Contents

1. Questions of Guidance   161
2. Our God Guides   166
3. Guidance and the Bible   185
4. Subjective Guidance   200
5. Guidance and the Church   217
6. Circumstances and Common Sense   227
7. Conditions for Guidance   236

Further reading   244

1

Questions of Guidance

Young people long to know what God's purpose is for their future. What professional calling should they follow? Should they go overseas for a short spell to gain wider experience? Some feel called to 'full-time' ministry either in their own country or overseas, but don't know how best to prepare for this calling.

We visit many churches and Christian Unions both in Britain and in other countries. As a result many people come to us to ask questions or share personal problems. It seems inevitable that we frequently face questions concerning guidance.

Throughout our lives all of us constantly have to make decisions which involve guidance. Is it right at this stage to change our job, or move house? Which church should we link up with locally? Should we join a rather stagnant local church or travel a few miles to a warmer Bible-teaching fellowship? As we begin to earn more, so we have more money to give away: what missions, Christian workers or other causes should we support? As the years go by we seem to have an ever-increasing list of prayer needs presented to us: should we concentrate our prayers on a few or pray generally for the many? Likewise there are more and more calls upon our time. I know this is a problem for our family. What should be the balance between family or home responsibilities and the pressing calls of Christian ministry? And which areas of ministry should have priority? Whatever our situations all of us will constantly face decisions of different sorts in which we as Christians need to know the will of God for us.

Meet Elizabeth

At the time, each issue seems tremendously important and we earnestly try to hear the voice of God. And it is true that often apparently quite small decisions actually affect the whole future course of one's life. Thus Elizabeth delayed her university studies a year in order to help her parents in the old people's home which they ran. If she had not done this, she would have gone overseas as a missionary a year earlier and we should perhaps not have met each other. So that relatively minor decision to help her parents actually altered the whole course of her life.

On the other hand, we often feel that God's overall guidance of our lives has been more important than the little details of specific issues. As we look back over what God has done for us, we praise him more for the broad sweeps of his paint brush than for the more detailed shading day by day. In fact, our weakness and sin has meant that we have often failed the

Lord and disobeyed him in particular matters, but nevertheless, we are gratefully aware that this does not deflect God from his overall leading of our lives. It is such a reassuring and comforting truth to know that with our gracious Father even 'if we are faithless, he remains faithful', *(2 Timothy 2:13)*.

It's not easy!

Some years ago I was invited to a large youth conference where the other main speaker was a powerful and gifted communicator.

He was a real man of God, but I had very definite doubts about his message. Having carefully defined his use of the word 'miracle' as an act of God which was not according to the natural order, he then stressed that every Christian should experience such supernatural miracles every day. I too believe in a God who works miracles. My wife and I have frequently experienced the Lord's gracious working of miracles. But we cannot say that this is a normal daily event for us. I wondered what this speaker's emphasis would mean for the young Christians listening with open hearts to what he said. Quite a few of them were new believers and some were insecure and unstable personally.

With these deep questionings in my heart, I discussed the matter with one of the other leaders at the conference. This conversation gave me a further perspective on how miracles can be a part of God's leading. We quickly discovered that our Christian lives had followed quite different paths, but came to the same conclusion. Both of us had to learn to walk by faith *and* sight. He came from a somewhat Victorian Christian home which was very godly, strong in biblical teaching and morally upright. But he grew up with little experience of the more direct working of God – and miracles were almost anathema! Now, as a mature Christian leader, he was beginning to move into what were for him new areas of faith. He was seeing God working miracles in answer to believing prayer.

Meet Martin

My background was different. When I first became a committed Christian at university, my knowledge of Christian matters was negligible. I was thrilled with my new faith in Christ and his saving work for me, but the tree of my faith lacked deeper roots. Was it all just psychological? Does God really exist? Does the cross of Jesus really deal with our sins? Did Jesus really rise from the dead? My joyful exuberance in Christ could be easily uprooted and shattered. But the Lord met me more than half-way. He worked miracle upon miracle in answer to prayer. When I prayed, things happened. When I asked the Lord for guidance, the way ahead became crystal clear. It was marvellous to see the reality of God. My God was alive and at work.

But as I have gone on in my walk with the Lord, my prayers have not always been answered in such spectacular fashion. In fact, often it appears that they have not been answered at all! And as I get older, it seems to become less easy to discern the will of God in specific decisions and I need to use what is sometimes called 'sanctified common sense'. I feel that God has been saying to me, 'In your early days as a believer I allowed you to walk by sight, because you were so weak. Now you must learn to walk by faith'.

Wherever you are in walking with the Lord, this book is written out of the conviction that God wants to guide you and all his people today. Our prayer is that everyone who reads the following six chapters will come away with a deeper sense of assurance and calling in whatever situation they are in. We do not know our readers individually. But God does. His love and care for each of us is personal and precious. That's why Jesus is often called the 'Guide' or the 'Good Shepherd', the one who died for us, his sheep.

Over to you

You will find it very helpful to write answers to these questions, rather than merely think about them.

1 *Can you trace God's overall guidance of your life?*
2 *Have you faced the need for direct guidance recently? If so, how did you expect God to show you his will? And did he?*
3 *Have you ever experienced God guiding you through your conscience? Did you obey?*

2

Our God Guides

What principles or patterns of guidance can we find in the Bible? Who does God guide and how?

As on every subject, so in the question of guidance we need to be soundly based in Scripture which is God's word to teach and lead us. Our ideas on practical subjects need to be soundly biblical and not just based on experience.

The Scriptures reassure us that God does not simply bring us to saving faith in himself and then leave us to our own devices. No, he takes us by the hand and leads us graciously and safely through life. This does not mean that we miss the normal heartaches, problems or tragedies of life in a fallen world, but in all situations we have the assurance of God's guiding presence with us. Thus, in Psalm 32:8 God says: 'I will instruct you and teach you the way you should go; I will counsel you and watch over you.' The context of this verse is that David was going through 'a time of distress' which is also described as a 'rush of great waters' *(Psalm 32:6)*.

The Psalms constantly affirm this foundational fact that God leads his people. Psalm 48 concludes with this triumphant declaration: 'He will be our guide even to the end' (verse 14). The psalmist declares that this is the nature of our God for ever and ever. He says that we are to pass on this good news from generation to generation – God is our guide! Psalm 78 adds the further assurance that God guides us 'with skilful hands' (verse 72). We may marvel at the skill of a pilot bringing an enormous tanker through a shallow channel into port. I remember being guided by tribal Christians to a remote village. We struggled through thick jungle and over a high range of hills for many hours. I had no idea of the way, but I had every confidence in the guidance of my friends. God's guidance is even more certain and 'skilful' than that of any person. How wonderful!

Are you in a wilderness?

In Psalm 78:52 the picture used is that of a shepherd. God led his people 'like sheep', 'like a flock'. This imagery of God as our shepherd comes again and again throughout the Old Testament. The theme is taken up in the New Testament with Jesus as the perfect shepherd who knows his sheep and 'leads them' (John 10:3). The sheep know the voice of the shepherd, and trust him, so they 'follow him' when he 'goes on ahead of them' (John 10:4). Guidance is not just God speaking to us from afar and telling us what to do or where to go, but rather he himself leads the way and goes with us, both into the 'green pastures' and also in the dangers and sufferings of the wilderness. The shepherd not only guides, but also leads from the front.

Jesus himself knew this amazing experience of being led in the wilderness. In Luke 4:1–2 Jesus was led 'by the Spirit . . . in the wilderness'. For Jesus there was apparently no contradiction between being in the Spirit and in the wilderness. Although he was in Satan's territory assailed by fierce temptation, he was still 'in the Spirit' and was being led. In fact, this is the only place in the Gospels where it is clearly stated that Jesus was led or guided by God. God does lead his people and did lead his Son Jesus, but the leading of God is particularly to be experienced when we are in the wilderness.

The final book of the Bible, the book of Revelation, shows us, however, that the wilderness is not the end of the story. There is a promised land. In Revelation 7 we see into heaven itself. We meet those 'who have come out of the great tribulation' (verse 14) and are now before the throne of God where the wilderness sufferings are ended. The Lord 'will guide them to springs of living water', he 'will wipe away every tear from their eyes' (verse 17).

It is good to be constantly reminded that our God does guide. He leads us even in the wilderness – in fact, particularly in the wilderness. His ultimate purpose and aim is to bring us into his glory.

Hand in hand with the Father

In the Old Testament only Israel really experiences the guidance of God. The New Testament emphasizes that the God of Israel wants to have people of all races and types as his children. *All* who receive Jesus Christ and believe in his name can now become children of God. No longer does our relationship with God depend on our background. We can be born again as children of the heavenly Father, 'not of blood nor of the will of the flesh nor of the will of man, but of God'(John 1:13). Men and women of every race, every class, every educational background can have God as their father.

Paul links the fact that we are children of God with the further truth that we are led by God's spirit (Romans 8:14). It is a sure mark that we are God's children if we are led by his Spirit. It is God's Spirit who gives us the assurance of intimacy with God, so that we can call God 'Abba, Father' like a child with his daddy. A father has special responsibility for his children.

I sometimes watch the married students at the college where I teach. It is heartwarming to see a father happily cuddling his baby or proudly leading his little child by the hand as they walk through the woods.

In my tutorial group I had a young mother who often fed her baby during our group worship times. It was beautiful to see her joy as she smiled into the face of her suckling child. We see something of God's relationship to us through the picture of human parents and their children.

God is our loving Father. He cares and provides for us. He teaches us what is right and wrong in his sight. He protects us. He leads us and takes us by the hand as we walk through life.

Again we notice in Romans 8 the dual context of our being led by the Spirit of God our Father. We do not escape the reality that we shall 'suffer with him'. But again the goal is that 'we may also be glorified with him' (verse 17).

God's overall guidance

Later we shall look at how God guides us with regard to specific decisions. But at this stage we want to look a little at the overall purposes of God into which the details of daily life must fit. It is hard to find God's will in these smaller matters if we do not understand the fundamentals of God's character, the way he works and the sort of things he desires.

We have sometimes enjoyed watching people playing the 'husbands and wives' game at parties or on television. 'What would your husband say, if . . .?', 'What would your wife do, if. . . ?', 'Does your husband/wife like it when you . . .?' Such questions depend on a married couple living together and sharing in such a way that they know each other's minds. We have now been married for nearly 40 years and often know what the other is thinking or feeling without any need for words. Likewise in our relationship with God it is good to walk closely with him so that we gradually learn what sort of decisions please him. We need to be steeped in the

Our God Guides

Scriptures which reveal to us the character and mind of the Lord. We are not only reading the Bible in the hope that we may get a direct 'word from the Lord' relevant to life now, but also to store up an understanding of God's ways. Then we may be able to make daily decisions in accordance with his overall will.

When children are small, parents need to give specific instructions on every detail of life. As children grow up within the family, they learn what patterns of behaviour are expected. They can then begin to think out right answers for new situations without needing to be guided in every matter by their parents. New and immature Christians may need specific words from the Lord on minor issues of behaviour, but hopefully we will mature and grow in knowledge of God's overall will for his people.

For example this 'mind of Christ' (1 Corinthians 2:16) applies to the choice of a life partner for marriage. Of course we want definite assurance from the Lord before we decide to get engaged. But we also want to ask more general questions. We know from the Bible that we are not to be 'mismated with unbelievers' (2 Corinthians 6:14 RSV). We don't, therefore, need guidance as to whether we should have a serious relationship with a non-Christian. God's will is clear. We know people who have taken a liking to a non-Christian and then have gone to the Bible in the hope that they might find a verse which may encourage them to go ahead with the relationship. Then they often twist the meaning of a verse to suit the guidance they wanted. Or they may go from Christian friend to Christian friend asking their opinion concerning this possible relationship. Eventually they will probably find someone foolish enough to say what was desired. They then reassure themselves that their decision was supported by other Christians. Actually they did not need to look for guidance at all – God's will was clear and obvious from his word. It was clearly 'No!'

What is God's overall purpose for us?

'This is the will of God, your sanctification' (1 Thessalonians 4:3, RSV). Paul is talking in this passage about how we 'ought to live and to please God' (4:1). He then outlines basic principles of behaviour by which we can judge individual matters. These are the 'instructions we gave you through the Lord Jesus' (4:2). Obedience to these moral instructions is for Paul the test of whether we are walking in the Spirit or disregarding the Holy Spirit.

As we look for guidance we see that there is an overriding principle that God's will for us in every matter is that we should grow in holiness, to be more and more like the Lord himself. 'But just as he who called you is holy, so be holy in all you do . . . "Be holy, because I am holy" ' (1 Peter 1:15–16). The New Testament constantly repeats this idea that we should be holy. One way of finding God's guidance then is to ask the question: what would the holy Lord Jesus do in this matter? If we base our reactions, words and deeds on the pattern and character of the Lord, we won't go far wrong. Likewise we shall study the Scriptures and learn from them what sort of thing is pleasing to the Lord, so that we can base our lives on the teachings of the Bible.

'I chose you and appointed you to go and bear fruit' (John 15:16). Here we see a two-fold purpose in God's calling of us. He has appointed us to go and to bear lasting fruit.

When Jesus called his twelve disciples it was not only 'that they might be with him', but also 'that he might send them out to preach' (Mark 3:14–15). Both in John and Mark the disciples are appointed by the Lord for an out-going, fruit-bearing ministry. They are 'sent out'; they must 'go'. In Mark 3 the necessary command to be with the Lord in close fellowship forms the preface to their being sent out. If they are to go out and bear fruit, they need to spend time in intimate relationship with their Lord and in learning at his feet.

Too often we Christians separate these two inseparable elements. Some of us are deep in our devotional relationship with the Lord, love to rejoice in prayer, praise and worship; but then we may be quite weak in evangelism. Others of us may be dynamic in evangelistic outreach, but know nothing of quiet meditation at the feet of Christ. The disciples are called to both functions.

It is of considerable significance that Jesus' disciples are not only called to live the life of God, but also are sent out to preach the good news. We too are disciples of Jesus and he sends us out also. We do not need special guidance to assure us that we are to go out into the world in witness. We may need some guidance as to where we are to go and exactly what strategies of evangelism we are to adopt there, but we know from the Bible that we are called to go.

'. . . fruit that will last' (John 15:16). God's purpose for us is that we shall bear fruit. We may wonder what sort of fruit is referred to in John 15. Is it the fruit of people responding in faith to the witness of Christ through us? Or is it the fruit of the Spirit, that lovely catalogue of spiritual qualities which we shall manifest if the Holy Spirit is at work in us (Galatians 5:22-23)? Perhaps it is both.

We are called to move out into all the world to bear fruit for Christ. The New Testament emphasizes God's saving purposes for all nations. The ultimate goal of our life and witness is that people 'from every tribe and tongue and people and nation' (Revelation 5:9) may worship the Lord. God's guidance for our individual lives should fit into his overall purposes for the world. We are not just individuals; we are also part of the history of God's church throughout the world and throughout history.

Our out-going witness to the world needs to be linked to the fruit of the Spirit as listed in Galatians 5. These beautiful characteristics of holiness are the result of being 'led by the Spirit'(Galatians 5:18) – so the guidance of the Spirit cannot be divorced from living a life with the fruit of the Spirit. We are not only to come into the experience of life in Christ by the Spirit, but we are also to go on into the daily experience of walking by the Spirit. Spirit-led guidance will lead us into the fruit of the Spirit (Galatians 5:25).

Our God Guides

And again we are reminded that John says that this fruit should abide. God is not interested in mountain-top experiences which do not last. May God give us a holiness of character which lasts and which grows! We may judge a true work of the Spirit by what it produces five or ten years hence. When it is God who leads us, he never leaves a job half-done. When he is our guide, he takes us through every testing to the end.

So we see that there are overall principles concerning God's guidance, but these do not always include specific leading for every occasion. Just sometimes God may see fit to give more detailed guidance. Thus for the building of the temple God gives very specific instructions concerning every detail of the construction, leaving nothing to the free will of the builders. But this is not usually the case. At Creation God tells Adam and Eve to 'multiply and fill the earth and subdue it'. He commands them to have dominion over all the animals. But he does not fill in the details of how to accomplish these rather general commandments. Likewise the Old Testament gives wise overall principles concerning social behaviour in the state of Israel, but many details of daily economic and agricultural life are left to the discretion and wisdom of the people. God gives us considerable freedom of scope for individual self-expression. He does not treat us as robots. He often trusts us to make responsible decisions on the basis of his overall purposes revealed in his Word.

How do we know God guides?

God is very gracious to us and treats us all in an individual manner. He does not stereotype the way he guides us. He suits his guidance to our individual situation, character and background.

The prophets – tailor-made guidance. The call of Isaiah contrasts sharply with that of Jeremiah. God takes the highly gifted and self-confident Isaiah into the impressive temple building. Here the great Isaiah begins to feel how puny he really is! He is given a vision of the Lord himself in majesty, 'high and lifted up' (Isaiah 6:1). Then he observes the flashing, burning seraphim flying about in the temple and calling to each other, 'Holy, holy, holy . . .' As if all that were not enough, God then causes the whole building to shake from the foundations up and the house is filled with smoke. Any pride or sense of self-sufficiency in Isaiah is surely knocked out of him by this fearful combination of events! No wonder he says, 'Woe is me! . . . I am ruined! For I am a man of unclean lips . . .' For the golden-mouthed Isaiah all this is a necessary prelude to hearing the voice of the Lord speaking to him, calling and guiding him into a prophetic ministry. Isaiah has to learn that God walks with people who have 'a contrite and humble spirit' and his reviving and renewing work is also for those who are humble (Isaiah 57:15).

Unlike Isaiah, Jeremiah was lacking in self-confidence. He had a low image of himself and his abilities. He was stalked by a depressing awareness that everyone was against him. Such a man would have been destroyed if God had led him into the temple for the sort of experience that Isaiah had. He would have had a breakdown. But God graciously guided him in a much more gentle fashion which was more suited to his nature. God's key word to Jeremiah was 'I am with you and will rescue you' (e.g. Jeremiah 1:8, 19).

With Ezekiel God's word came in the form of strange visions. God matches the forms of his speaking to our personality and character. Not everyone would appreciate the apocalyptic vision given to Ezekiel. But Ezekiel realized that somehow this 'was the appearance of the likeness of the glory of the Lord' (1:28). This caused him to fall prostrate before the Lord and then to hear the Lord actually speaking. Is this a pattern for guidance? When we are deeply conscious of God's overwhelming glory and fall in awe and humility before him, then we are in a right position to hear God speaking to us.

God met Amos while he was busy in his daily work as a shepherd. As Amos says, 'the Lord took me from tending the flock' (7:15); Amos was 'one of the shepherds of Tekoa' (1:1). And the Lord suited his message to Amos' background – his prophecies are full of earthy agricultural imagery.

Both with Amos and Habakkuk God's word seems to have come in some visible form. Amos 1:1 talks of the words which the prophet *saw*. And Habakkuk 1:1 says 'The oracle of God which Habakkuk the prophet *saw*' (RSV). It is true that the Hebrew word for 'oracle' is rather uncertain in its meaning and may well have the sense of 'burden'. Habakkuk *saw* the burden which lay heavily on the very heart of God and in the following verses the prophet utters a cry to the Lord which echoes God's own heart cry. So the call of Habakkuk comes by *seeing* into the mind and feelings of God. His ministry then fits into that understanding. When we really grasp the heartfelt purposes of God, we are called to align our lives to them. God's leading then comes through this understanding of the mind of God.

God suits his leading and calling to us as individuals. Guidance is not always easy to describe. I personally do not find it easy to say how the Lord has led me in different situations in my life. One can rationalize his guidance and over-simplify it, but actually one knows that all sorts of factors played a part in the fact of God's guidance.

For this reason I have been much impressed by the beginning of Jeremiah and Joel – 'the word of the LORD came to me' (Jeremiah 1:4; Joel 1:1). The Hebrew actually means 'the word of the Lord *was* to me'. It is meaningless in Hebrew, as it is in English. We want to ask immediately *what* the word was to Jeremiah or Joel. It seems to make no sense just to say that the word *was* to the prophet. But surely that is just the point. When we try to describe how the Lord's word of guidance or call really became clear, it seems so complex, and yet it came with assurance. We know the Lord has spoken to us, but all descriptions of how he led us seem trite and over-simplified. Often we just have to come back to this somewhat unsatisfactory biblical idea that the word of the Lord just *was* to me. Bad grammar may sometimes be good spiritual truth!

Our God Guides

From the experience of the prophets, then, we can see that God suits his methods of guidance to the situation of his servants. Don't expect *your* guidance to come just like someone else's!

So let's look further at some of the many ways God led other people in the Bible.

Exodus – one step at a time. If we look at the book of Exodus, we see God leading Moses and guiding his people out of slavery in Egypt through the years of wandering in the wilderness and on towards the promised land of Israel. In chapter 2 comes the story of how Moses' sister was given wisdom in how to get the baby Moses back to the care of his mother. She had hidden him from the murderous designs of the Egyptians and concealed the baby in the bulrushes. In this story there is no mention of God at all. God allowed Moses' sister to use her own sharp mind and wise common sense.

In contrast to this we have the following chapter with the story of the burning bush. Here God begins his guidance through the miraculous sight of a bush burning without being consumed, but goes on to speak directly in a conversation with Moses.

In Exodus 5 Moses and Aaron become God's instruments to bring God's word of direction to Pharaoh. They pass on to him the Lord's word that he should let Israel go. But Pharaoh points out that he does not know the Lord and will not heed his voice (Exodus 5:2). Then God speaks to Pharaoh through the series of plagues which he miraculously causes to fall on Egypt. But miracles alone are not enough. Pagan magicians can also do miracles – and the wise men of Egypt did in fact match many of Moses' miracles. Still today animistic spirit mediums, Hindu priests and the leaders of some Muslim mystical movements perform healings and other miracles. God does use miracles to introduce us to his word, but miracles alone are not an infallible evidence of truth.

We today can look back at the story of Israel's journey through the wilderness to Canaan, but at the time the people could only see one step at a time. In Exodus 17:1 they 'set out . . . travelling from place to place as the LORD commanded'. God often leads us in this way. We cannot see beyond the next step. Israel found this very difficult and Exodus 17 continues with Israel faithlessly complaining in rebellion against God and Moses.[*]

When we were called together to missionary service in Indonesia, we assumed we would stay there until old age. After less than three years, we returned to our home country for furlough and then the Indonesian political situation prevented us from going back there. God moved us on to Malaysia and then to Singapore. In the same way we had assumed that our call to serve with the OMF in Asia was for our lifetime. In fact, after ten years it proved right to move on to our next work at All Nations Christian College. Guidance is sometimes like driving without knowing the route, but being guided by someone in the passenger seat. They instruct you to follow the signs to some town and you think you must be going to that town. But after a while they redirect you to some other place. And so it goes on until you reach your actual destination. God may lead us by stages, one step at a time.

So far we have seen some fundamental principles of guidance illustrated in Exodus. We also note that God spoke often in an audible voice to Moses. He led Israel too in the visible form of the pillar of cloud and fire. We are bound to ask then whether God still guides us normally in such clear, tangible fashion. Christian mystics like Margaret Kempe have traditionally talked of the outward and the inward ear. Sometimes God may speak audibly so that we actually hear him with our ears, but normally we hear his directions through the inward ear of our conscience, our mind or our intuition. The very overt forms of guidance which were normal to Moses seem to be less common today. Perhaps Moses and the Old Testament saints needed this more specific guidance. They did not have the full Bible as we have it today, but just some oral traditions concerning the dealings of God with their forefathers.

Moses had relatively little understanding of the nature of God. Only in Exodus 6 did he first come to know the gracious covenant name of God *Jehovah* and it was even later that he was given the Law which is a lamp to our feet and a light to our path (Psalm 119:105). But still it is clear that even today God may lead his people in overt audible or visible ways. If he sees that we need such clear and direct guidance, he can grant what we in our weakness may need. It does not seem, however, that this is the norm now.

Acts – natural and supernatural. In the Acts of the Apostles God guides his people in a whole variety of ways. And sometimes the apostles simply proceeded without direct guidance from God so that it is just recorded that they did this or that. This is underlined by such words as 'he determined to return' or 'intending to' do something (Acts 20:3, 7, 13).

As with Jesus, so with the apostles, their movements were often determined by what was their normal practice. In Acts 17:2 Paul follows his master's footsteps and starts his ministry in Thessalonica by going to the synagogue 'as was his custom'.

Sometimes guidance came through other people. But it was not always leaders who did the sending. In Acts 17:10 'the brethren' sent Paul and Silas away to Beroea. In 15:36–41 Paul and Barnabas both had ideas of what they wanted to do.

Circumstances played a vital part. Through persecution the Christians were scattered throughout Judea and Samaria, preaching God's word (Acts 8:1). It was through Jewish opposition and Gentile openness to the word that Paul and Barnabas were moved to begin preaching to Gentiles rather than the Jews only (Acts 13:44–46). This was confirmed to them by their knowledge of the Scriptures (Acts 13:47).

But the book of Acts does also tell of direct guidance by the Holy Spirit. So in 13:2 and 16:6 the Holy Spirit speaks directly. In 8:26 and 27:23 it is an angel that speaks. It would seem however that there is a close connection between the angel and the Spirit, for the guiding word of the angel in 8:26 is immediately followed by the Spirit speaking to Philip in 8:29.

Our God Guides

Sometimes in Acts guidance comes also through more sensational means. Dramatic visions are given to Peter in Acts 10, to Paul in 16:9 and to Ananias at the conversion of Paul in 9:10. In 18:9 the Lord again speaks to Paul in a vision. We notice in 16:10 that the vision to 'come over to Macedonia and help us' evidently needs some discerning understanding, for they 'conclude' or 'infer' that God is calling them to preach the gospel there. It is apparently not immediately obvious. They have to think the vision through and interpret it.

In counselling with students at All Nations who have been given visions, I have sometimes noted that the vision may not be literally fulfilled, but it sets the student moving in certain directions.

In the New Testament church there were some people with a specific calling to be prophets. They played a part in the giving of God's guidance. In Acts 13:1 it was prophets and teachers through whom the Holy Spirit spoke to call Paul and Barnabas for special missionary work. Then in 21:10–14 there is the strange story of the prophet Agabus who foretells Paul's sufferings if Paul insists on going up to Jerusalem. This leads the Christians to beg Paul not to go, but he pays no attention to the prophecies and confidently asserts that he is ready to die for Jesus. Paul knows that God has called him to go to Jerusalem and will not allow himself to be turned aside from God's call. But doubtless, Agabus' prophecy would remind him that his sufferings in Jerusalem and then in Rome were within God's purposes for him and under God's control.

One guide – different voices

God's methods of guidance vary according to the situation and to the person being guided. He graciously matches his dealings with us to our needs. We must not try to narrow down God's amazingly diverse patterns. We should also be careful not to consider one way of guidance more 'spiritual' than another. God may lead some of us in overt and dramatic fashion; others he may expect to use our sanctified common sense and our fundamental knowledge of Scripture. This may also vary from one stage of our Christian life to another. But whatever may be the methods of his guidance, we rest in the confident assurance that God does carefully lead us through life. He is our Father and our shepherd.

Over to you

1 *What is your experience of a father? How does this influence your view of God as Father and his guiding your life?*
2 *How can we develop a Christian mind-set? Be specific.*
3 *Can you identify with one of the prophets? If so, read again Isaiah 6, Jeremiah 1 or Ezekiel 1 and apply it to yourself.*
4 *List the ways God gave guidance in the Acts of the Apostles.*

3

Guidance and the Bible

The Christian Union meeting was over. Coffee loosened the tongues of the students as they stood around chatting together. A little group gathered round me with questions.

'At the end of this year I finish my time here,' one said, 'and I have no idea what I should do next.' Another student chipped in: 'Yes, it's so difficult to know what God wants us to do. I've only been a Christian six months and I don't know what to do about my girl friend. She's very tolerant about my becoming a Christian, but she doesn't want to have anything to do with Christians or Christian ideas. I like her a lot, but . . .' His words drifted into a silence which spoke eloquently of his deep uncertainty.

'Yes, but it isn't only those big decisions,' commented another person. 'As a Christian you want to do the Lord's will in all things, but how do you know what is to God's glory in the little decisions of everyday life?'

How encouraging to see the keen determination of these young Christians to please the Lord in all things! I sympathized so much with their longing for quick and easy solutions to the whole question of guidance.

I began to tell them about our marriage relationship. In the early days we loved each other very much, but actually didn't know intimately how the other one ticked. Sometimes therefore we failed to do what our partner would really have liked. But our relationship in love was more important than the details of what we did or didn't do. Sometimes we needed to say to each other, 'I love it when you . . .' or 'I find it annoying when you . . .' But gradually we have grown to know each other more fully and we feel instinctively what would please or displease.

Words and the Word

'But that is precisely the point,' one of the students exclaimed with some impatience. 'How can we get to know God in such a way that we do appreciate what he wants in a particular situation?'

'Well, I suppose the Bible . . .' began another person, only to be interrupted quickly by a woman wearing very fashionable clothes, 'The Bible is great, but you can't get life from a book. Words, words, words – the world is full of words! But you can't trust words. You can twist words to make them mean whatever you want. Surely God has got some better way than just words.'

I began to explain that actually God does use words, but not in a dishonest way. Right from the outset of history God has acted through words. It was when God spoke that creation took place. In Genesis 1 it comes again and again, 'God said, "Let there be . . ." .' And when God spoke, things happened. John's Gospel picks up this theme when it says, 'In the beginning was the Word.' It also states that all things were created through the Word. It was actually in and through the Word that there was life. In fact John boldly equates the Word with God himself (John 1:3, 4). So we have to be careful not to denigrate words, for God himself is identified with 'the Word'. And God creates through his Word.

Some people say, 'What's in a word?', and the answer surely must be that *words bring results*. This is especially true of God's 'word', the Bible.

Words and God's will. God's word is creative and active. It is also a word that reveals. The Old Testament is full of references to God speaking to his people and to his prophets. 'Thus says the Lord'; 'The Lord said to him . . .'; 'The word of the Lord came to me, saying . . .' Again and again God speaks to people in order to reveal his character and nature as well as his desires and purposes. These words became part of the written word of God, the Bible. God himself wrote the Law on tablets which he then gave to Moses to bring down to the people of Israel. God caused his revelation of himself in word and in historical actions to be recorded in the written word of the Bible. This written word became the ultimate authority in all matters and the source of a true understanding of God and his ways.

Words and the character of God. Through study of the Bible we learn the nature of our God. We then submit all uncertain questions to the test. Is this idea in line with what we know of the character of God? Is this course of action likely to please God and bring honour to him? Does this form of worship fit what we know of the holiness and grace of God? Through the Bible we grow in our understanding of the Lord himself. This then enables us to know whether a particular doctrine, form of spirituality or course of action would please him.

Our guidance is based primarily on God's self-revelation in the Bible rather than almost magically subjective bits of guidance. We shall look in a later chapter at subjective guidance which can also play a part in showing us God's will for us, but it will always be subject to Scripture and so to our overall knowledge of the character of God.

I want to emphasize this fact that guidance is based on the knowledge of the character of God. Perhaps I can best do so by contrasting the ideas of revelation in Islam and Christianity. In Islam revelation is fundamentally aimed at showing the will of God rather than helping people to know God himself. Islam does define certain characteristics of God in the so-called '99 most beautiful names of God', but there is also a strong sense that God is infinitely glorious, high above mere humanity and powerful. He is therefore above all description. He is also so removed from us that we cannot really relate to him intimately, like a child to a parent. The aim of revelation is then to tell people what God wants them to do in worship, prayer and service. It is sometimes

Guidance and the Bible

said that the *Qur'an* is like a sign-post telling us the way.

Christianity is so different. God's word not only reveals the will of God, but above all it shows us God himself in order that we may know him, love him and worship him. This will of course result in joyful obedience and service because we are grateful to him for all he is and all he has done for us. Because we know him, we can also know his will for us. It is that way round.

Hear the word

So God's written word is our authority in all matters. What is not clearly found in Scripture cannot be authoritative. The Bible alone has authority over us. All forms of subjective guidance must be submitted to the test of Scripture. Even the guidance of Christian leaders does not have ultimate authority. And although we are not to be rebellious Christians who easily reject the words of our leaders, we are to put their words to the test of Scripture and thus to our knowledge of the nature of God himself. Christian leaders will surely play a part in our guidance. But they do not have final authority over us and we must not just follow blindly what they say. Guidance comes from our knowledge of the Bible above all else.

Words and pictures. Some people react to such an emphasis on the Bible because they say 'The Bible is just words. You can't trust words.' After all Jesus used visual aids to get across his teaching. He instituted the visible symbols of bread and wine.

Yet words are essential to *explain* the meaning of signs. And it should be added that even signs in the Bible have been handed down to us through the written words of the Bible. Even the Jewish Passover tradition needs words. Jews share the Passover meal in their families with many symbolic actions and special foods which have significance. But during the meal the story of the original Passover is retold and thus passed down from generation to generation.

In the Christian Lord's Supper the symbolic eating and drinking of bread and wine means little without verbal teaching on the sacrificial death of Jesus.

God may therefore use other means of speaking to us besides words, but his primary method is through his word. This impresses us in the New Testament. Jesus and the apostles use words to show people God and his ways. Old Testament passages and verses are the proof of truth. As we have seen, when Paul makes his dramatic decision to begin mission among Gentiles, he supports the rightness of this by quoting words from Isaiah (Acts 13:46–47).

The key word. But the New Testament is not just talking about the use of words to show people God and his will for us. The key to the New Testament is Jesus himself. And he does not just speak words – he *is* the Word. How can we play down the significance of words when our Lord himself is the Word? Let's

Guidance and the Bible

be careful before we swallow slogan thoughts like 'actions speak louder than words'. God reveals himself in the person of the Word, Jesus the Messiah. Through this living Word we can know the Father – Jesus 'has made him known' (John 1:18). 'He who has seen me has seen the Father' (John 14:9). Through Jesus, the Word of God incarnate, we can so know the Father that we shall understand his will. Jesus follows the will and purposes of God the Father (John 5:30; 6:38). If we base our lives on the example of Jesus, we too shall not stray from God's desires for our lives.

The word of God creates and reveals. It is 'living and active ... discerning the thoughts and intentions of the heart' (Hebrews 4:12). And what does Paul say about the Scriptures in 2 Timothy 3:16–17? They are 'useful for teaching, rebuking, correcting and training in righteousness, so that the man of God may be thoroughly equipped for every good work'. What is guidance? Surely, it must include teaching, reproof, correction, training in righteousness and being equipped for the good works which God wants in our lives.

The word of God, incarnate and written, forms the basis of our Christian lives. If we want to know the will of God in any situation, we shall examine the example and teaching of Jesus as recorded in the Bible. We shall also study the whole Bible, the written word of God, to learn what pleases God and what arouses his anger. On the basis of biblical teaching we may then make sound decisions, praying that God's Spirit will help us to apply the Scriptures and the principles of the Bible to our particular situation. So how can we do that?

Making sense of the Bible

Get it in context. 'Wives, submit to your husbands as to the Lord . . . the husband is the head of the wife as Christ is the head of the church' (Ephesians 5:22–23). These verses are sometimes quoted to support a chauvinistic male domination in the home. Such a misuse of the verses not only fails to understand the real meaning of 'head' and 'submit', but it also takes these verses out of context. Paul goes on to show in what way Christ related to his bride, the church. He so loved the church that he sacrificially 'gave himself up for her'. This passage is not talking about male supremacy, but of mutual subjection. The husband does not lord it over a submissive wife, but follows the example of Christ in being her 'suffering servant'. If taken out of context, Bible verses can cause problems.

When we use a Bible verse, we should check its context.

Find the true sense. We were listening to a cassette about the life of Samson. The speaker on the cassette recounted how Samson only regained his strength when his shaven head grew a new crop of hair. The cassette applied this story to us today. If the church develops new forms, it will manifest the power of God. New songs, new forms of worship, new structures in the people of God; these are the essential conditions for new power by the Spirit.

We smiled at each other at this point. 'No,' I said, 'this passage tells us that the church lost its power when it allowed the old forms to be shaved off. We must put away new songs and other modern innovations. When the old hair is allowed to grow again, then we shall have power.'

We laughed. Neither interpretation related at all to what Judges 16 is really talking about. Such use of Scripture is dangerously fanciful. We must stick to the true sense of a passage. Otherwise we may be seriously led astray in our personal lives and in the development of our churches and fellowships.

When we come to the Bible, we must always ask what this section of Scripture really means. What did the author intend to convey? What did the original readers centuries ago understand the passage to mean? Only when we have asked such questions can we look to the Holy Spirit to apply the words to us and our situations today. We need to be very careful of a fanciful or allegorical use of Scripture.

Get behind the scenes. In Islam the *Qur'an* is said to have been written by God on a tablet in heaven before all time. The *Qur'an* is the uncreated and eternal word of God. Its contents are not formed in any way by the prophet, nor are they culturally conditioned at all. Such theology is radically different from the Jewish and Christian belief. Our Bible is not only inspired by the Spirit of God, but also written by people in particular cultural and historical contexts. As we read any particular book of the Bible, we immediately notice this. For example, we may compare the book of Jeremiah with Luke's writings in his Gospel and Acts. It would be ludicrous to suggest that Jeremiah might have written Luke's Gospel or that Luke might have penned the prophecies of Jeremiah. They are written in different languages –

clearly aimed at different people and coloured by the personal character of their authors.

'The Bible says . . .' is not necessarily an infallible guide in life. We sometimes need to look at the background of a verse and see what it meant in its original cultural context. 'If your hand or your foot causes you to sin, cut it off . . . if your eye causes you to sin, gouge it out' (Matthew 18:8–9). I observe that a literalistic understanding of this verse is not popular even to those who claim always to follow the 'plain sense of Scripture'! How few blind Christians without hands or feet there seem to be! Literalism may lead us into trouble in our Christian lives.

With this in mind, we need to come again to some of the controversial issues of church life. Should women cover their heads when praying? Should women be allowed to preach, teach or pray aloud in public? What does the Bible teach about ordination by the laying on of hands? Or about tithing? Or about a day of rest on the Sunday?

Our lives are to be guided by God's revelation in the Bible. To achieve this we need to do our biblical homework seriously. Biblical passages should be kept in context, understood in their true sense and not fancifully. We then want to try to discover the significance of biblical teaching in the light of the cultures and ways of thought of biblical times.

Logos and *rhema* – a double act

'The Bible only gives us general principles of behaviour. It does not really tell us what to do day by day.

Guidance and the Bible

We need more specific guidance than that. God should tell us clearly whether this particular person is his chosen partner for us. Should we apply for this work or training course? That is the sort of guidance which is important.'

'The Bible is only a book. A book-religion lacks real life. Paul says that the written word kills. It is the Spirit who gives life (2 Corinthians 3:6). For guidance, as indeed for every side of the Christian life, we have gone beyond just the Bible. We have the Spirit.'

Such quotes highlight a grave danger in the church today. The unique place of the Bible as the supreme revelation of God and of his will yields ground to other more subjective forms of guidance.

Some Christians today are making a false distinction between two Greek words used in the Bible for 'word'. *Logos* is thought to mean the ultimate, objective word which stands above everything, while *rhema* is said to be the more living, direct word. *Logos* may therefore be the ultimate test of orthodoxy and truth, but it lacks immediate relevance and life. *Rhema* is both inspired and inspiring. It speaks directly to us and to the actual needs of the moment.

Logos, such people believe, is of course the word of God found in Scripture. *Rhema*, they think, may take various forms. It may be a verse or passage of the Bible which the Holy Spirit particularly highlights and brings to life in order to speak to us. It may also be a word of prophecy or a word of knowledge quite separate from Scripture.

But if *rhema* is the living word of God apart from Scripture, then the Bible in practice takes second place in our lives.

However, in the New Testament itself *logos* and *rhema* seem interchangeable. If, for example, we look at Luke 4:22, 32, 36 the direct speech of Jesus is said to be *logos*. His words (*logoi* verse 22) are 'gracious' as he describes his own future ministry in Luke 4:18–19. Then in Luke 4:32 his *logos* astonishes his hearers because it is 'with authority' – surely then not some remote or unrelated objective word! And then in Luke 4:36 the *logos* of Jesus commands the unclean spirits and casts them out. It is not only in Luke that the *logos* of Jesus has direct miraculous power. In John 4:50 an official's son is healed by the powerful *logos* of Jesus.

On the other hand *rhema* stands not only for a direct prophetic word of power, but also for the gospel in general. In John's Gospel it is *logos* which creates all things, while in Hebrews 1:3 *rhema* upholds the whole universe. The New Testament includes dozens of references both to *logos* and *rhema*. Anyone taking the trouble to look at the New Testament usage of these two words will see immediately that there is no distinction between them.

It sounds spiritual to contrast the objective word of Scripture with the dynamic living word applied to specific situations, but the Bible itself does not encourage this. The word of God, *rhema* and *logos*, reveals the character of God *and* his will.

Bible verses for you

In the old days some Christians picked a card out of their 'promise box'. On it was written a verse with a

Guidance and the Bible

promise. Many have found guidance in this way. Later the 'promise box' gave way to the set verses of Daily Light. Or a calendar with a verse for each day hangs in the toilet to guide us through the decisions of the day. Other Christians may open their Bible at random and a verse leaps into focus – this must be the word of God for us today.

Such a use of Scripture borders on magic. Dangers abound. We have to remember that the Devil also uses Scriptures. Matthew 4:6–7 shows Satan and Jesus in spiritual combat, both using biblical verses as their weapon. In the question of guidance it is right that we should use verses from the Bible as our means of discovering God's will, but we must not assume that the Bible can be used like some book of magic formulas. We should check that Bible verses are kept in context and in their true meaning. And we shall want to compare the guidance a verse gives us with the overall teaching of the Scriptures.

At various times in my life I have found God leading me through a verse of Scripture. I was not expecting or looking for a verse to speak to me, but the Spirit made a word from the Bible stand out. These were memorable and exceptional occasions at times of particular need. At one time I had been fighting God's call to missionary service overseas. At another I felt God was stopping us returning to Indonesia because he had something else in store for us.

God used a Bible verse to speak to us in a special way on another occasion too. We were in Indonesia at the time. The communists were very strong in their opposition to us. They picked on something I had said in a church elders' meeting and determined to take us to court for high treason. The penalty for this would be life imprisonment. The Indonesian legal system was terribly corrupt in the early 1960s and we knew we stood no chance of a fair trial. And our local prison was no holiday centre! It had no running water and prisoners did not normally have the chance to wash or use a toilet. The smell was indescribable. I lost my peace as I contemplated a life-time in such a situation. I could not sleep. My mind went round and round without any rest. Prayer seemed futile.

In my distress God spoke. One morning I read Psalm 125:2, 'As the mountains are round about Jerusalem, so the Lord is round about his people'. If the Lord protects Jerusalem, no enemy can penetrate the wall of mountains around her. Was this not also so for me? I desperately asked the Lord to be like a range of mountains around me. From that day the communist party just forgot about their planned accusation against me. The whole affair slipped away.

God may indeed speak to us and guide us by Bible verses.

Bible verses for groups

Guidance does not only come to individuals, but also to groups of Christians together. A verse of Scripture may also take on significance for a whole church. I remember a few years ago our college principal started the academic year with the verse 'the glory of the Lord filled the house' (1 Kings 8:11). For all of us on the staff and among the students this verse became the Lord's word to us and the theme of our prayers. As a college we longed that God's glory might so fill our buildings that even casual visitors would sense God's presence. We were much encouraged when various visitors and students' parents commented that they could feel God's presence as soon as they entered the front hall. God had led us as a college to know what to pray for.

God's word 'is a lamp to my feet and a light to my path' (Psalm 119:105). Psalm 119 teaches us that God's word shows us the right way in which we are to walk. It asks how young people can keep their way pure and affirms, 'by guarding it according to thy word' (verse 9). By storing up the word of the Lord in our hearts, we can be kept in God's ways of purity and preserved from the sin of false decisions (verse 11). The key to guidance is found in the Bible.

Over to you

1 *What can we do to encourage more understanding of how to interpret the Bible in our church or Christian Union?*
2 *What can we do to deepen our own personal knowledge of the Bible?*
3 *Has God used a Bible verse to guide you personally, your church or your Christian Union? Look at that verse again and study it in its context. Does it still guide you in the same way?*

4

Subjective Guidance

**'I felt the Lord was saying to me that I should ...'
'The Lord led me to ...' 'I knew this was God's word
to me'. 'God called me to ...' How often I have
heard testimonies which have included such statements! The obvious question is, 'How?'**

We noted in chapter 2 that God varies his guidance
according to our individual character and situation.
He guides in many different ways and it is impossible to categorize his methods too neatly. In practice
we find that God does not only speak to us through
his word, the Bible. He has many different ways of
showing us what his will is. But it must be constantly
underlined that all subjective forms of guidance
should be submitted to the test of Scripture.

Get the message – God does guide

Before we begin to look at specific ways in which
God leads us, it is good to remind ourselves first of
the glorious truth that we can trust God to lead us

step by step in his ways. We need the guiding hand of God, for otherwise we shall surely go astray. Wayward sheep need the constant care of a shepherd. God alone knows what is best for us and he graciously leads us. He has perfect plans for our lives and longs to show us his will. And it is so reassuring to know that his will is 'good, pleasing and perfect' (Romans 12:2).

First, the will of God is good. God's predetermined plan for our lives is morally upright. He desires that we should be holy as he is holy (Leviticus 11:44–45; 1 Peter 1:15–16). God's leading will never be morally questionable, nor will it lead us into compromising or sinful activities. Holiness is a fundamental characteristic of our God and it is a basic factor in his guidance of us. He wants us to grow in holiness.

Second, the will of God is pleasing. In Victorian times it was taught that God calls his people to sacrifice. He would generally insist on us doing what we least want. 'Death to self' was the motto. There was little emphasis on a God of love who delights to lavish good gifts on his children. Today in unhappy homes the title 'father' may conjure up all sorts of unfortunate images. But Paul reassures us that our heavenly Father's will for us is 'pleasing'. God is not an ogre.

Third, Paul reaches the triumphant climax. The will of God is 'perfect' – and in the purposes of God there is nothing superior to perfection. 'Perfect' is perfect! God does indeed have a plan and purpose for our lives. And there is nothing better than God's will for us. So we can walk with God in confidence.

Paul shows too that God has made us and brought us to new life in Christ with a specific intention. We are to produce those good works which God planned for us 'that we should walk in them' (Ephesians 2:10, RSV).

Yes, there are quite specific things he calls us to do for him, for his church and for his world. It is not just an academic truth that God has a definite purpose and calling for each one of us. He now challenges us to set out on the pathway he has designed for us. At every stage of life we need to discover what good works God has in mind for us personally and 'walk in them'.

Although Ephesians 2:10 clearly teaches that God has detailed plans for our lives, we may not always need specific guidance on every point. We need not look for clear guidance on which shirt we wear today. If we wrestle in prayer on every tiny decision in daily life, we shall end up with a nervous breakdown. God may give us a strong sense of guidance even on the tiniest decisions, but normally we can just walk in the Spirit and trust God to lead us according to his purposes. This is the life of faith.

Actually, of course, it sometimes happens that an apparently insignificant decision can have major repercussions. For example, I have a pullover from Peru of traditional Peruvian Indian design. One day a group of young Peruvians saw me wearing it. Through this we soon got into conversation and I was able to share Christ meaningfully with them. As we walk with the Lord, he guides us even in tiny matters like the choice of which pullover to wear! We can trust him to guide us without us even sensing his direction in such matters.

But the more important the decision, the clearer we shall want to be about the Lord's will for us. For example, in the choice of a life partner.

How then does God make his will known to us on particular issues?

The mind of Christ

I love the verse in Philippians where Paul says that 'God is at work in you, both to will and to work for his good pleasure' (2:13 RSV). There are four stages in the action of this verse: God works in us; we want that which pleases him; we then do the work he wants; finally comes the climax that he gets pleasure from it all. But it all starts with God working in us and shaping our wills so that we long to please him. We begin to desire what he desires, to like what he likes. It is no longer a struggle between our selfish, proud aims and the gracious promptings of the Spirit. Our minds and our wills are attuned to what God wants.

When students ask me about guidance for the future, I often ask them, 'What would you really like to do?' If I get an answer which shows a selfish or materialistic outlook, then I want to challenge them to get right with the Lord before they worry too much about guidance. But if they are clearly wanting the will of the Lord and to live for his glory, then my question can be very helpful. 'I would love to work among Muslims in North Africa,' a bright young woman said to me recently, 'but am I the right sort of person for that? And I am not sure of God's call.' I suggested that it might be the Holy Spirit who was at work in her giving her that desire.

So I encouraged this woman to move definitely in the direction of missionary service in North Africa. God would confirm the rightness of it by giving her his peace. But if we were misreading the will of God, then he could easily close the door for her. If we genuinely want to obey him, God will not allow us to go astray.

It might be wise at this stage to add a small word of warning! When it comes to the question of boy/girl relationships, we need to be rather more cautious. In chapter 6 we shall look at some of the things we should look out for in guidance about a life partner.

The peace of God

In Colossians 3:15 Paul exhorts his readers, 'Let the peace of Christ rule in your hearts.'

I remember how I felt before God called me into missionary service. I was studying modern languages at university and people began to say to me, 'Keen Christian plus linguist equals missionary.' I felt their mathematics was false. Many Christians are keen on languages without necessarily being called to overseas mission. I denied their logic. I did not want to be a missionary. God had not called me, I maintained.

Subjective Guidance

But I began to lose my sense of peace with God. My prayer times seemed cold and unreal. As I considered the future, it lacked purpose and appeared so unclear. Life lost its joyful vigour. God was showing me that I had wandered in my plans onto the wrong track. It was only when I realized God's call and surrendered to his will that God's peace returned to me.

Of course, we can lose our peace for other reasons. An undisciplined lifestyle with inadequate sleep can lead to headaches, mild depression and loss of peace. Purely physical problems may steal our peace from us – a persistent cold, nagging asthma or a bout of 'flu. Women may find that they temporarily lose their peace at a particular time of the month. When we talk of God's peace being a factor in guidance, we are not talking of such temporary and human matters. We mean a long-term and continuous lack of peace where God seems to be disturbing our nest and pushing us to fly in new directions.

We should not rush into a new calling without first testing this sense of loss of peace. Don't abandon your studies in your enthusiasm over a challenge to full time service. Don't walk out on your job because of bored dissatisfaction or some difficulty in relating to your boss. Don't flit from church to church in a search for the ideal spiritual fellowship. Butterflies don't make good Christian workers!

The peace of Christ in Colossians 3:15 is linked to the following verse: 'Let the word of Christ dwell in you richly'. The word for 'dwell' gives the idea of God's word making its home in us. So let the word of Christ richly indwell you. Let God's word in the

Scriptures so fill you and permeate your thinking and your attitudes that God can then guide you by his peace.

Signs from above

Deserted army barracks surrounding a huge tent became the base for a linguistics course for missionary candidates. It was here that we first met. We sat opposite each other the first evening at supper. I fell in love on the spot.

Elizabeth was the girl I wanted, but was this really God's will? We were both heading for missionary work with the same mission in the same part of the world. But I wanted to be sure of God's leading. I asked God to give me signs. 'Lord, let me meet her on my way to the kitchens' – and, sure enough, she happened to be there! 'Lord, arrange for us to be in the same class, if you really mean us to be together for life' – and so it worked out! In his grace, God gave me sign after sign to encourage me to persist in my love for Elizabeth.

It is rare in the Bible that God looks for his people to ask for a sign. There is no evidence in the New Testament of people asking for a sign but God may, however, give signs to confirm the reality of his work. In Luke 2:12 the shepherds were given the sign of 'You will find a baby wrapped in cloths and lying in a manger.' This confirmed to them that God had indeed sent the Saviour, the Lord and Messiah. So also in the early church, the truth and reality of their preaching was confirmed by signs and miracles. In

Mark 16:20 it is clear that the signs follow after the disciples go out to preach the word. The signs were not a starting point for faith or guidance, but God gave them to demonstrate the spiritual authenticity of the words. The New Testament Christians do not seem to have asked for signs as a means of guidance.

We read in the Gospels and 1 Corinthians that the Jews frequently asked for a sign. Jesus rejected their demand and pointed out that it is an evil generation which wants a sign. 'Jews demand signs' (Matthew 12:39), but Paul affirms that he will only 'preach Christ crucified' (1 Corinthians 1:22). Paul refused to pander to their desire for signs.

Of course it is easier to know God's will if he will grant us concrete signs.

As I look back to those days when I asked for clear signs to confirm that Elizabeth was God's chosen partner for my life, I realize just how immature I was. Perhaps God saw that I was spiritually weak and immature, so I needed visible signs. In his grace God always gives us what we need.

Visions and dreams

In the Old Testament God frequently spoke to people and guided them by means of dreams.

Paul often received God's guidance through a vision, while Joseph and the wise men from the east saw dreams at the time of Jesus' birth. (The Bible seems to make little or no distinction between visions and dreams, *e.g.* Numbers 12:6).

Does God still speak to people in this way? Yes! A young Scottish friend of mine was working by his machine on the factory floor one day when he suddenly saw a vision of Jesus telling him that he should become a missionary to Asia. My friend was not only converted that day, but set his face towards missionary service in Asia.

A few years ago I visited East Malaysia at a time of sweeping revival. It was challenging to be asked to discern the meaning of many dreams which people had received. Sometimes the message was clear, sometimes it seemed impossible to know what it meant. But one could not deny the reality of visions.

It sometimes happens that a picture comes into our minds as we are praying or waiting on the Lord. Such pictures can be a beautiful gift from God to make his will clear to us. Of course, like all visions and dreams, pictures can come from three different sources – from God, from Satan or from our own natural minds. Visions call us to exercise the gift of discernment and should be particularly tested by the standards and teaching of the Bible. If the picture or vision leads us to unholy living or to unbiblical emphases in our teaching, it is certainly not from the Holy Spirit.

The Bible constantly warns us not to be unduly impressed by the spectacular. Even signs and wonders can come from false prophets and may even lead the elect astray (Mark 13:22). And certainly dreams, visions and mental pictures are unreliable channels of God's guidance unless carefully tested by the standard of the teaching of Scripture and the holy purity of God.

Prophecy today

What exactly is prophecy? It may be a word from God foretelling the future. In the Old Testament it often did tell in advance the details of the coming of the Messiah, the judgment of the nations or some future event in history. But prophecy is also a message inspired by the Holy Spirit applied to particular needs or situations. It may be a word of rebuke, encouragement or exhortation.

Dreams and visions were part of the pentecostal fulfilment of the prophecy of Joel 2:28, and Acts 2:17 says that 'your sons and your daughters shall prophesy'. When God pours out his Spirit, we can expect that Christians will be inspired to prophesy. Prophecy is mentioned also in Romans 12:6, Ephesians 2:20, 3:5, 4:11 and Revelation 10:11. In 1 Thessalonians 5:20 Paul commands us, 'Do not despise prophesying.'

And the ministry of prophecy did not cease with the writing of the New Testament but continued on in the church for many years. The gift was particularly common in the churches of the Middle East and among the monks and ascetics of Egypt and the desert areas.

But gradually the gift of prophecy was no longer recognized in the church. Was this because the church had lost its vitality? Or does God only pour out on his people the gifts he sees to be needed by them at any particular time in history? It seems more likely, however, that this spiritual gift was in fact practised throughout Christian history, but not known by that name. People may have called it 'inspired teaching/preaching' or 'a word from the Lord' and failed to see that actually it was prophecy.

I find this answer more acceptable than to suggest that the church lacked spiritual vitality for so many centuries. I do not think that we today are more spiritual than our forefathers!

Is prophecy God speaking? Does prophecy hold the same weight and authority as Scripture then? Those who emphasize the biblically untenable distinction between *rhema* and *logos* would tend in practice to equate prophecy *and* Scripture as 'The word of God'. Thus, Bruce Yocum in his book on prophecy states that prophecy is 'almost like listening to a tape-recorded message'. Many feel that prophecy is indeed God's very words relayed to us. I query this. The Bible alone is God's perfect word. Only in the Bible does God's Spirit so inspire people and overrule their fallible human nature that their words are actually God's unadulterated word. Prophecy, like preaching and teaching, should be God-inspired, but the message still comes through the mediation of the speaker.

In Scripture, we believe that this human mediation was so directed and overruled by God's Spirit that the Bible is God's perfect word. But I do not believe that this is the case with prophecy today. The sin and weakness of the speaker will distort and corrupt the message, so that it is fallible. The hearer will need therefore to use discernment in testing the message, sieving out the human corruption of God's message and then obeying what is seen to be God's word to us.

The impression that a prophecy is literally the direct words of God is enhanced by the use of the first person singular, as in the jargon formula, 'My little children, I . . .' It would be better to say, 'I feel that God is wanting to encourage/warn us that he . . .'

If a prophecy comes in the first person singular, it seems that we dare not criticize it. God's own words are above discernment! Surely we can only humbly submit and obey. But if the prophecy comes in the more modest third person with the assumption that it comes through a fallible human being, then we can happily exercise discernment.

How can we tell it's true?

a) It must be in accord with the teaching of Scripture and the character of God revealed in the Bible and in the person of Jesus Christ.
b) It should lead to the hearer exalting the basic truths of the Christian faith.
c) Careful assessment by other Christians who are accustomed to speaking in a prophetic manner (1 Corinthians 14:29).
d) The test that Jesus gave in Matthew 7:16: 'You will know them by their fruits'. Galatians 5:22–23 lists nine aspects of the fruit of the Spirit. A prophet's life should show holiness, spirituality and sound doctrine.
e) If a prophecy is predictive, then we should watch carefully to see if it is fulfilled.

Some Christians were excited a while ago by prophecies that the four million Soviet Jews would come out from Russia through Scandinavia to Israel. This would happen in the middle or late 1980s, some said. There was a partial fulfilment in the exodus of many thousands, but it is still only a relatively small minority – and did not involve Scandinavia.

The genuineness of the prophet's gift will be seen in the fulfilment or non-fulfilment of his or her words. In the Old Testament the penalty for false prophecy was stoning. This may sound extreme. But to speak in the name of God is no light matter.

Who should discern prophecy?

a) Other people with prophetic gifts. In 1 Corinthians 14:29 Paul says, 'Let two or three prophets speak, and let the others weigh what is said.' It is very possible that this verse is suggesting that prophecy should be tested and discerned by other Christians who have the same prophetic gift.

b) All believers. Paul goes on to say that 'all can prophesy one by one'. He seems to be opposing the idea of some élite circle of people with a special prophetic gift. The whole body of Christians has the spiritual responsibility as well to judge whether a particular prophecy is a genuine word from the Lord.

c) Church leaders. In some churches a Christian is not allowed to give a word of prophecy unless it has first been submitted to the church leaders. And yet all Christians are a 'royal priesthood' (1 Peter 2:9) with direct access to the presence of God through the shed blood of Jesus. Because of the sacrificial death of Christ for our sins, we can all know God personally and intimately, hearing his voice to us and discovering his will. We must not surrender these precious privileges by making our leaders into mediators between God and ourselves. Jesus is our one and only mediator; we need no other, for he is totally adequate.

But Christian leaders do have the responsibility to set an example to their flock and to teach the word of God. They should therefore lead their people in the exercise of the gift of discernment, helping the congregation to test the biblical validity of prophetic words. In their leadership they should have the courage to say openly if for some reason they do not think a word of prophecy is genuine.

There is a particular problem here in groups of young or inexperienced Christians, such as school or college Christian fellowships or Christian Unions. The leaders may not be mature enough to shoulder this responsibility. In such cases Christians would be well advised to be particularly careful before naively accepting prophecies or visions. If problems still remain, it may be wise to call in a mature Christian leader for advice.

The relationship of prophecy to guidance is not easy. Clearly God does want to speak to us in relevant ways which apply to our particular situations. His main method of speaking is through the Bible. But he also uses prophetic preaching, teaching and Bible exegesis. Other prophetic utterances can play a part too in showing us the will of God when we face decisions.

Some Christians today are amazingly gullible in naively accepting so-called prophecies as God's word to them. Other Christians are so sceptical and critical that the Spirit may easily be quenched. The Christian walks on a tightrope.

Words of knowledge

The Spirit may also give us a word of knowledge, in which he makes us aware of things we could not otherwise know. It is not easy to distinguish this from a natural gift of wise discernment, but it should be said that the so-called 'natural' is also God's creative work in us and therefore need not be so separated from spiritual gifts. Likewise, it is not always easy to distinguish between a word of knowledge and just a hunch or feeling. This is particularly difficult if the word of knowledge or hunch is not absolutely specific. 'Somebody in the meeting tonight has toothache' – it is more than likely in a good-sized meeting that there will be somebody with toothache!

In the exciting movement of God in Timor, Indonesia, in 1965–68, Christians were told by God to do evangelism in a particular village – the name of which they had never heard of before. Then they were told the name of the man there whom they were to contact and to whom they were to preach the good news of Jesus. It was very specific.

Philip's story. In Acts 8 Philip was told to leave Samaria and go to a desert road. Philip did not

Subjective Guidance

hesitate to obey this somewhat subjective word of guidance (Acts 8:27). We might deduce from this that God looks for immediate and total obedience without careful sifting when we hear a word of guidance. But perhaps we need to notice various factors in the story before we apply it too quickly.

We know from Acts 6 that Philip had been chosen for the humble ministry of serving tables because he was a person 'of good repute, full of the Spirit and of wisdom' (Acts 6:3). He was therefore not only filled with the Spirit, but also morally upright and known for his wisdom. He had also shown his humble faithfulness by serving tables while others had the up-front preaching ministry. Such a person may readily discern the word of the Lord.

Philip was a person who so knew the word of the Lord and the mind of Christ that he was happy to go down to Samaria to preach to these non-Jews without any specific guidance at all. From his knowledge of Christ and the Scriptures he knew that the gospel should be preached not only to Jews, but also more widely to the Samaritans (Acts 8:5). Knowing that this was within the purposes of God he went down to Samaria without waiting for guidance. This was the sort of person who was able then to react immediately to the angelic word of guidance (Acts 8:6–8).

We notice that the angel's guidance led him away from the revival work of Samaria to the barren situation of the desert road. He was led away from the glamour of the crowds to the obscurity of a lone Ethiopian eunuch. How rarely subjective guidance today seems to lead us away from the spectacular and sensational to the unsung solitude of the desert!

Over to you

1 *How can we know the difference between natural loss of peace and the divine umpire's work of guidance?*
2 *Study Colossians 3:12–17 and Philippians 2:1–13, putting Colossians 3:15 and Philippians 2:13 into context.*
3 *If you hear what claims to be a word of knowledge or prophecy, how do you judge/discern its message?*

5

Guidance and the Church

The barracks hummed with eager debate. The barriers between officers and men yielded to the uniting pressure of this major decision facing them. Should the whole battalion turn to Jesus Christ and be converted to the Christian faith? Most of the men were convinced that Jesus Christ could give them a new life which would transform the whole atmosphere of their army life.

But some objected. Some Muslim soldiers felt there could be problems with their families. Others were not sure that the Christian life fitted the rough-and-tumble of the army. All knew that they needed a new pattern of relationships. Finally the decision was taken. The way ahead was clear. Officers and men together submitted to the authority of Christ. As the poet Arthur Clough says, 'There is a great Field-Marshal, my friend, who arrays our battalions.' The whole battalion underwent instruction in the Christian faith and then gave their allegiance through baptism to their new commander.

What's in a group?

In many cultures overseas it is customary for decisions to be taken by groups of people together. The lock-stock-and-barrel conversion of this army battalion was not unique in Indonesia. I had the joy one day of leading a whole hospital ward to Christ. Soon after we left the country a senior school of five hundred teenagers was converted.

Such group decisions relate not only to conversion, but God's guidance may also come to groups of people together.

All of us in our families have indulged in such debates. Finally a general consensus of opinion emerges and a decision is taken. If this group discussion takes place with prayer, surely God will lead us to the right decision by his Spirit. Committees work on this principle. Debate ranges around a matter until finally the Spirit leads to a communal decision. Is this what happened in Acts 15? Peter spoke first, followed by Barnabas, Paul and finally James. Finally 'it seemed good to the apostles and elders...' (Acts 15:22). It had also been through a group decision that Paul and Barnabas had been set aside for wider missionary service in Acts 13:1–3. The Holy Spirit said, 'Set apart for me Barnabas and Saul...'

Some British churches today are doing something very similar. They see a town or housing estate with little live Christian witness and determine to plant a new church there. Church planting is better done by a team of Christians resident in the locality, so that local people can actually see the people of God living and worshipping together.

The established church therefore separates several of its members to move house into the target area and start the new church.

Who decides which Christians should move house and start the new work of evangelism or church planting? Unless the church is exceedingly autocratic, it cannot simply tell people to move house and start a new church elsewhere. The people concerned will need to be consulted. They will then prayerfully consider the suggestions put to them before agreeing to them – or rejecting them!

'Guidance by consensus'. Guidance may come through the church as a body or through the leadership of the church, but it must then be checked by any individuals concerned.

In the mission to which my wife and I belonged we called this 'guidance by consensus'. Within the basic principle there was considerable room for flexibility. When we joined our mission in 1960 the emphasis was on guidance through the leaders. So they interviewed us when we first arrived in Singapore and then, after considerable prayer, tentatively designated us to work in a particular country. We were then asked to pray through their suggestion and hopefully put a tick to it.

Today the emphasis has shifted. New candidates to the mission are asked to discover from the Lord where he wants them to work. This sense of call is then submitted to the leaders of the mission, who will agree it if at all possible. But there is still the same basic idea that the Lord leads both the individual missionary and also the leaders of the mission together.

If two agree

'Barnabas took Mark'; 'Paul chose Silas'; 'Paul wanted Timothy to accompany him'; 'the brethren sent Paul and Silas away by night'; Paul 'called to him the elders of the church'. It seems that *all* Christians at that time were open to receive their guidance through the mediation of other believers.

If two Christians agree in asking for something in prayer, then it will be given to them. And if two or three are gathered in the name of Jesus, then he is specially present with them (Matthew 18:19, 20). So also in guidance there is the assurance of Jesus' presence when Christians gather together. It is wise therefore for individual Christians to meet with other Christians when we face serious decisions.

This has two advantages. First, we are specially aware of the Lord's presence when we are in a group like that, so it seems easier to hear his voice and determine his will. Second, we find that each of us has different insights which can be added together to bring combined wisdom to the situation.

I am often amazed how apparently very unclear situations have become so very obvious when we have come to the Lord in such groups together.

A local church may have a pastoral committee to help members facing personal problems or a missionary committee to advise people who are wondering about Christian service overseas. Otherwise individual Christians may ask a few respected Christians who know him or her well. They may then meet together to discuss and pray about the situation in order that they may find the mind of the Lord.

It is of course wise to ask for such help from older and more experienced Christians who are known for their wisdom and spirituality.

Love your local church. When Christian leaders sense the Lord's guidance and feel that they are discerning the ministry which some Christian ought to begin to exercise, they should gently suggest this to the person. They will not presume to tell him or her that their suggestion is a definite word from the Lord which must be obeyed, but will tentatively put the proposition to the younger Christian and ask him or her to pray about it. In this way the will of God may be shown to a Christian through church leaders or other believers.

Individual Christians today will often face the situation of having various groups of leaders caring for them and offering them guidance. By force of circumstances we may belong to one church in our home town where our parents live, another in the place where we studied and a third where we now work. Students are often involved in CUs too, while missionaries have a responsibility to their society, sending church and national church.

As Christians we may look up to older believers in each of these and they may play some part in guiding us in the name of the Lord.

It is easy to talk in theory of the responsibility of the church to see the gifts and talents of their members, to help guide them in the Lord's way and to stand prayerfully with them in these questions of guidance and pastoral needs. But suppose the church does not have the spiritual life or vision needed?

One of my students felt strongly that he should not go overseas as a missionary unless his home church felt it right and agreed to be his sending body. But they did not have that kind of vision. They had no interest in mission overseas and felt no pastoral responsibility of that sort for their members. Many of us feel it right to play our part in witness within a local church which is not overflowing with spiritual life. We may not then be able to look to the church for help in guidance. Others of us may belong to churches which are too strong in their emphasis on authority and 'covering'. We may then face the tension between an unbiblical submission and a contrary independence of view which the leaders will not accept. Nevertheless we shall not want to slip into an individualism which does not allow us to find the Lord's will for our lives with the help of more senior Christians who know us well.

Don't go it alone

The rubber-tapper's dark little house stood at the end of the village on the edge of a large rubber plantation. The whole family had gathered together, the parents with their nine children plus grandparents, uncles and aunts. As pastor to the older children I too had been asked to attend this family gathering and give my opinion in the question to be debated.

Guidance and the Church

The father explained, 'We don't have enough money to educate all the children. The price of rubber is down. We can only afford now to have one child at school. The question before us is: which child?'

Everyone present shared their views and the final decision was clear to all. We were unanimous in asking the third child to continue at school, go on to university and study to become a doctor. The others left school the next day. One followed his father in tapping rubber, another became a petrol-pump attendant in a local garage.

From then on all watched the child at school. Today he is a fine Christian doctor, but who does his salary belong to? The family, of course! He owes everything to his family. How would the family react if he suddenly said he felt called to give up his career and become a missionary? Impossible! He cannot disregard the rights of his family and his responsibility to them.

Our guidance is never restricted to ourselves in its effects. The command of God does not say, 'honour your parents until you are eighteen or twenty-one.' We have the God-given duty to honour our parents even after we are mature adults. We cannot snap our fingers at our families, saying that we feel that God is guiding us in a certain way. We must always take our family into consideration.

In seeking God's guidance we are not just looking for our own satisfaction. Of course it is true that God has given us our particular background, gifts, talents and personality. He surely wants these to be fully used – he gave them to us for a purpose. Nothing is accidental; God is sovereignly in control of our lives from the moment of our conception. He surely wants us to be fulfilled through the proper exercise of all our gifts, but we for our part should not be selfishly aiming at our own self-fulfilment.

As we pray for the Lord's will to be made clear, we have two aims in mind – to bring glory to the Lord and to serve the needs of others.

Our primary goal in life is to glorify the name of the Lord. The Christian is saddened by the way God's name and the name of Jesus are dragged in the mud. The Christian longs to make it clear what the Lord is like and what he has done for us, so that people will come to love him, believe in him and give him the honour which is his due.

'. . . and your neighbour as yourself'. Our secondary goal goes inseparably together with the first. If we love the Lord our God, we shall also love our neighbour as ourselves.

When we wonder about a career or look for a job, we shall ask ourselves and the Lord how best we can be used to serve a needy world. We shall not be asking the world's usual questions about promotion possibilities, salary scale, job satisfaction or career prospects; rather we shall be asking whether this job gives scope for service to the church and to society. When we consider where to set up home, we shall not ask which area is nicest or which house is the best we can afford. We shall not just look for a home near a church which can feed us and give us happy fellowship. We shall ask ourselves where we can be of most use to the Lord and the church of God. Where can we be of service to needy people in our society? This should be the basis for our guidance.

Fitting into God's great plan. As Christians, we do not believe that we live independently of others. We are part of the total body of Christ throughout all ages and all over the world. In our guidance we shall also take this into consideration. Surely the Lord will lead us in such a way that our lives and ministries fit into the overall pattern of his working through history and throughout the world. How can I fit my ministry into the overall strategy of God in the world?

What is God wanting to do today? When I was a student there was a great burden on many hearts for the continent of Latin America which was at that time a rugged mission field with little evangelical witness. Today the situation has markedly changed. We now face the formidable challenge of the world of Islam. How can we fit our lives into that call from the Lord to his church? What will be the supreme challenge of God to his people in the next generation? Southern Europe?

God does guide individuals. But our guidance must fit into God's working in the wider circles of the church and of the world. Guidance is not just selfish without due consideration of others.

Guidance together

God guides not only individuals, but also groups of people together. When he does guide individuals, he may well do so through the church and through the wise counsel of more mature Christians who know them well. God's guidance of the individual not only touches the life of that person, but also has wider ramifications. We have to consider our guidance in the light of our wider responsibilities – to our families, the church and its needs worldwide, and the world in its suffering and injustice.

Over to you

1 *Which mature Christians could you turn to for help in questions of guidance? What natural and spiritual qualities make them suitable for this role? How well do they know you?*
2 *As you consider job applications, what motives are primary? List them in order of importance.*
3 *How could you best contribute to God's development of the history of the church worldwide? If you think this is too ambitious a question, what is your purpose in life?*
4 *How do you relate your personal sense of guidance to the wishes of your parents and family?*

6

Circumstances and Common Sense

The Bible comforts us with the strong message of God's sovereignty. He directs and controls the movements of the nations through history. His loving purposes graciously lead his people. He overrules the lives of individual believers.

We may expect therefore that he will so arrange our circumstances that we are gently pushed into the way he has planned for us. Sickness and physical weakness don't come by chance. The demands of infirm elderly parents are not accidental. Failure to find employment does not take God by surprise. God often uses such things to lead us in his way. When we are wondering about guidance, we should always take such circumstances into account, believing that our God reigns as Lord of all things.

Paul prayed that the Lord would open to him a door for the preaching of God's word (Colossians 4:3) and in Revelation 3:8 God assures his people 'I have placed before you an open door, that no-one can shut.' It is God who opens or closes doors for us.

He often uses natural circumstances towards this end.

A Swiss friend of ours had felt the call of God to missionary work in Thailand for many years. She patiently completed her medical studies, had a couple of years of professional experience, started her missionary training – and then discovered that she had an incurable back complaint. The missionary society could not possibly accept her with such an illness. We had to face the possibility that it was Satan preventing her from such front-line service. We prayed for her healing, but gradually the Holy Spirit gave us the sure conviction that God had other purposes for her.

She now has a rich and influential ministry in Switzerland, but her previous call to Thailand has given her a special love for that land. She prays fervently for others who work there. Her deep interest in Thailand is infectious, so God has used her to call others into missionary service there and into caring support in prayer and finance. And our friend's sufferings, as Paul affirms in Romans 5:3–5, have indeed produced in her a spirit of patient endurance, a depth of character and a confident hope in the Lord.

Open doors

If God graciously opens a door for us, we should walk confidently through it into the paths he has planned for us. If God closes a door, we should not fret or complain, but joyfully rest in the assurance that the sovereign Lord knows what is best. We have noted before that his will is 'perfect'.

It is not only true that God may use circumstances to lead us into his will for us. Equally he will confirm it through circumstances when we have made a decision in accordance with his purposes. 'We shall need a house; we have no furniture; what about our children's schooling? Our bank balance is nil; our parents need us; we surely won't be able to find a job there.' Our minds often go round and round worrying about all the problems. Sometimes it is hard to see how things will pan out, but the Lord is still in control. If we follow his leading, he will wonderfully make all our circumstances fall into place.

What if we go wrong?

But what happens if we make the wrong decisions? Do we have to walk through life with the depressing knowledge that we have missed God's best purposes for us? No! The sovereign Lord knows everything in advance. He knew before the creation of the world what we would be like and what decisions we would take. He is well able to overrule all circumstances, including our mistakes and our sins to bring blessing. 'We know that in *everything* God works for good with those who love him' (Romans 8:28).

We have experienced the reality of this. Our missionary career seemed to go wrong at every stage! We were designated to serve in Indonesia, but no visa was forthcoming. As a result I gained invaluable experience in South Thailand. Then we had under three years serving in the Indonesian churches before political developments prevented us continuing our ministry there. Later we moved with joy to a training ministry in Singapore, but soon faced the bitter disappointment of being asked to relinquish that work after just three years. Our leaders felt we had been inadequate. We certainly had made mistakes. But with hindsight we can see now how God was moving us towards our present work and preparing us for it in his perfect, gracious way.

As the Psalms declare, 'the steps of a man are from the Lord'. He will keep our steps steady on the right pathway. We need not fear! (Psalm 37:23; 119:133).

It is not only our outward circumstances which are under God's direction, but also the infinite and complex details of our background, personality and gifts. Our character and experience are given us by God for a purpose. As we face guidance decisions we should sensibly take into account these vital factors – what sort of people has God caused us to be? What training and experience has he led us into? He makes no mistakes.

The prophet Jeremiah had to learn this. In calling him to be a prophet God reassured him that 'Before I formed you in the womb I knew you, before you were born I set you apart' (Jeremiah 1:5). God determined to call Jeremiah to a prophetic ministry even before he was born. But Jeremiah still demurred and made excuses. 'I do not know how to speak, for I am only a youth' (1:6). Jeremiah pleaded his inexperience and lack of speaking ability. It sounded humble. But God was not impressed, for he had been preparing Jeremiah particularly for this ministry. God knew what background, gifts and experience to give Jeremiah in preparation for his call. So Jeremiah, despite his apparent humility, was in reality questioning God's work in and for him. The Lord therefore strictly commanded Jeremiah, 'Do not say, "I am only a youth" ' (1:7). He then told Jeremiah simply to be obedient and do what he was told, but with the reassuring promise that 'I am with you to deliver you' (1:8).

A close friend of mine once shouted angrily at me, 'It's all right for you. You don't have my background.' Actually her unhappy childhood had prepared her superbly for the particular social ministry which God had given her.

In looking for God's guidance it is important to ask: 'In his sovereign control over our personal development, what has he been preparing us for?'

Use common sense

God has made us in his image. He abounds in warmth of personality, not sitting coldly on some remote Mount Olympus as an unthinking, unfeeling Ultimate Reality. The Bible constantly affirms that God determines to do certain things. He has a mind and uses it. Created in his image, we too are called to think critically and make wise decisions.

Let us take the example of relationships. How do we know that one particular person is right for us? The Bible does give some fundamental principles. It makes it clear that we are not to 'be mismated with unbelievers' (2 Corinthians 6:14, RSV), for the apostle realistically points out that such mixed marriages between a Christian and a non-Christian lack any deep unity of heart. They will lack agreement on all sorts of subjects – use of money, choice of friends, what they do on Sundays and in the evenings. Indeed they will find that they serve different masters. What a recipe for disaster!

But the Bible does not tell us precisely which person is to be our life partner. How then do we discover God's will in this vital matter?

Your life partner

First, we want to be confident of love. Do both partners really love each other? 1 Corinthians 13 gives us some good tests. For example, 'love is not self-seeking' – is that true of our behaviour towards each other? Love 'always protects, always trusts, always hopes' – love causes negative criticism to yield to an optimistic faith in the other person. The apostle Peter says that 'love covers over a multitude of sins' (1 Peter 4:8) – rose-tinted glasses are a good sign of love! When Paul is talking about love in Philippians 2:3 he exhorts us to 'consider others better' than ourselves.

I well remember a young student coming to my study to discuss his growing attraction to a certain young woman. He said, 'I'm sure she couldn't be interested in someone like me.' It happened that the woman in question also came to see me on the very same day. She told me of her growing interest in the student who had just before been talking with me.

Circumstances and Common Sense

But she too doubted the possibility that he could be attracted to her, for she felt that he was far too good for her!

Love does indeed consider the other better than ourselves. It is important that we look up to our partner as somebody we are really proud of.

While love certainly involves a very definite physical attraction and a stirring of the emotions, it also includes personal friendship.

In choosing a life partner, we face some basic questions. Do we have everyday interests in common? Can we relate to the other's social or racial background? Do we have the same basic aims in life? There are three essentials: that we love each other; that we are confident of God's leading; that we can happily anticipate a life-time together in the everyday realities of normal life.

The New Testament makes it clear that love delights to give and to serve. The evidence and outworkings of God's love for the world was that he gave sacrificially (John 3:16). Jesus showed his love for us by taking the form of a servant for our sake (Philippians 2:7). The media's picture of love tends to be selfish. When a man sees a pretty woman he desires her for his own self-gratification and pleasure. But as Christians we believe that love longs for the welfare and happiness of the other. We long to give pleasure to our partner and to serve them humbly for their sake. That is the mark of real love. When wondering whether we really love someone or whether they truly love us, we have here a biblical test.

Conscience

In determining what course of action is right we shall not want to go against our conscience. In Romans 14:23 Paul declares that it is sin if we act with doubts of conscience and without faith. Having said that, we need, however, to recognize that our consciences are also part of our fallen nature. They need to be educated by the constant reading and teaching of the word of God.

In this chapter, we have stressed the importance of our God-given minds, wisdom and common sense. And yet, the sovereign and all-powerful Lord may overrule all our carefully determined plans and so arrange our circumstances that we are pushed into apparently less sensible ways. He knows what is right in his eyes, what is best for us and for the world in which we live. Even the apparent foolishness of God is actually wiser than all our human knowledge (1 Corinthians 1:25).

Many people today are sensing that purely human wisdom ultimately proves inadequate.

God is able

As Christians we are particularly aware that our common sense may not prove adequate to guide us through the maze of life's decisions. We have learned to doubt our own wisdom. Fortunately we do not need to resort to gimmicks or astrology or magic games with occult overtones. God has provided a better way. 'If any of you lacks wisdom, he should ask God, who gives generously to all without finding fault,' advises James, 'and it will be given him' (James 1:5). What a reassuring promise for weak mortals like ourselves! We can turn to God in humble prayer and he will give us his wisdom, so that our decisions will not be made all by ourselves. They will be made *with God*. He will so work in us that his wisdom will enter into our decision-making processes. Thanks to such prayer, in line with the promise of God, we can exercise our God-given responsibility to choose, to use our common sense and what wisdom we possess.

Over to you

1 *What factors in your background might be significant for your future life and work?*
2 *What experience and training has God arranged for you to have?*
3 *What gifts do you feel you have? What gifts do your friends think you have? How can these gifts be used for the glory of the Lord?*
4 *What are the marks and characteristics of Christian love?*

7

Conditions for Guidance

What is the will of God for our lives? All of us face a variety of calls upon our time. What are the priorities? It is easy to allow our diaries to become overfull without serious consideration of what God really wants us to be doing. What can we do to avoid this?

Prayer – get the habit

It may prove helpful to spend a day in quiet, unhurried prayer and meditation in the presence of the Lord. One after the other the various sides of our lives can be mentioned before the Lord and then in the silence we could spend as long as we wanted on each subject. Our minds might consider what a new meeting would mean for us – how many would we attend? How much time do they take up? Are they strategic? Do we feel at home in such meetings? Do we feel a sense of peace that this is God's calling to us? Should we then be doing more of this sort of work? Or less? At the end of a day of such meditation on the different aspects of our life we may well feel more confident of the will of God for us.

In the New Testament fasting is not just a spiritual discipline to teach us self-control, but it is closely associated with prayer. Prayer and fasting together in unhurried fellowship with God can unravel many knotty problems. The way ahead may become clearer.

As we pray, we are expecting God to mould our thinking to fit the patterns of his will for us. As we saw earlier, the Christian mind is formed by the teaching of Scripture. Our prayer, therefore, will be based on our overall knowledge of the mind of Christ as seen in the Bible.

As we pray about our lives it may prove helpful to consider what God has done through history. It is often said that history repeats itself. This is certainly true in the saga of church history. And yet many today are praying about their relationship to their church without any consideration of church history. With a reasonable knowledge of the subject we may be able to pray with greater insight and so come to wiser decisions.

Many of us have been stimulated and guided in our prayers by the example of other Christians. Biographies of significant Christians may provide direction for our prayers. How did God lead them? What was their experience of the Lord and his dealings with them? We may ask the Lord in prayer what lessons he wants us to learn from men and women whose life-stories have been written up for us.

Humility first

We should not think that God will only guide us if we fulfil certain preconditions. And yet it is also true that the Bible teaches some principles which may facilitate God's guiding word being heard.

King David points out in Psalm 25:9 that God 'guides the humble in what is right, and teaches them his way'.

As we acknowledge our weakness and need of the Lord's loving guidance, we shall be more likely to hear his word to us. The same Hebrew word for 'humble' is also used in Psalms 76:9 and 149:4 which declare that God gives his salvation to the meek. Amazingly too it is the meek and humble who will inherit the earth (Psalm 37:11, Matthew 5:5). Humility is a basic precondition for salvation, guidance and a ministry of influence in the world.

Obedience and forgiveness

Psalm 25:9 leads on in the following verse to the affirmation that the Lord's 'ways' are full of love and faithfulness for those 'who keep the demands of his covenant'. We cannot expect the Lord graciously to guide us unless we are willing to be obedient. Such obedience will surely issue out from a genuine love for the Lord mingled with a deep sense of awe. Proverbs 1:7 points out that 'the fear of the Lord is the beginning of knowledge'. Such humble obedience may be seen as a middle path between self-will on the one side and a masochistic desire for sacrifice on the other.

'I want' is not a good beginning to a prayer for guidance! 'Lord, show me your will for my life. I'll do anything for you as long as it is not . . .' No, we come before the Lord with our lives open before him.

The aim of our life is to glorify the Lord. As Paul says, 'you are not your own; you were bought with a price. So glorify God in your body' (1 Corinthians 6:19–20).

Many of us have a fear that this means God is likely to call us to do what we most dislike. If there is one thing we really don't want to do, that must surely be the Lord's will for us! As we have seen, our heavenly Father is not like that. He loves us very dearly and delights to lavish good gifts upon us. He is not an ogre who revels in torturing his people.

So the Christian should be open to the Lord for whatever he desires. All of us need constantly to say to the Lord, 'I will do anything for you and I will go anywhere you want.'

Sometimes the Lord will surprise us, so we need to be flexible in approach. Jonah was a good Jew and it never occurred to him that God might send him to preach to Gentiles, but he did. If we are too rigid in what we expect from the Lord, we too may get a shock or two! Be ready for anything in the service of the Lord!

Perhaps the greatest hindrance to guidance is sin. When we are consciously living in disobedience to the revealed standards of God, we cannot expect his voice to lead us clearly. Sin blocks the ears.

When prayer is easy, then guidance also grows clearer.

Be practical

Some of us were brought up on the old slogan '*Ora et labore*', 'pray and work'. It is often true that prayer should lead to active practical outworkings. In seeking God's guidance, too, our humble prayers may well need to be linked to some practical steps.

When my wife and I returned to Britain after two terms of missionary service, we were very unsure of what would be our next step. Various openings were offered to us, but nothing seemed right. The months slipped by with all the heartache of uncertainty. It was at this stage that an older friend and Christian leader wrote to us, saying, 'God cannot steer a stationary ship. You need to go ahead and do something positive.'

It is often good to take definite steps to discover more information about the way we could take. When wondering about a job, find out more about training courses, job opportunities and what life would really be like. It may be right to actually apply for particular posts and see what doors open.

Patience, advice and pieces of paper

As Christians we believe that God has a specific path prepared for us. It is unseemly therefore to engage in a feverish search for an open door (Isaiah 64:4).

God 'works for those who wait for him'. Sometimes it's right to stand back from a frenetic search for God's will and wait patiently and prayerfully for the Lord to act on our behalf.

We are called to be fellow-workers with Christ, and not just passive objects.

It is hard to know how to pray when we face difficult decisions, particularly when our emotions are deeply involved in the decision. We may find it helpful to write down on paper what possible paths could lie ahead, or make a list of the advantages and disadvantages for each possible choice. This may facilitate intelligent prayer as we seek the will of the Lord.

How to be a living sacrifice

We have already observed how Paul firmly believed that God's will is 'good, pleasing and perfect' (Romans 12:2).

There is a neat symmetry in the first two verses of Romans 12: 'Therefore, I urge you, brothers, in view of God's mercy, to offer your bodies as living sacrifices, holy and pleasing to God – this is your spiritual act of worship. Do not conform any longer to the pattern of this world, but be transformed by the renewing of your mind. Then you will be able to test and approve what God's will is – his good, pleasing and perfect will.'

Because A is true, therefore do B; do C and thus experience D. A and D are closely related, as are also B and C. In diagrammatic form:

A	in view of God's mercy,	*therefore do —*
B	offer your bodies as living sacrifices,	*do —*
C	be transformed by the renewing of your mind.	*and thus*
D	what God's will is.	*experience —*

Paul appeals to us to present our bodies 'as living sacrifices'. As with sacrifices dedicated to the Lord in the temple, so our bodies are to be holy. In the service of Christ there can be no easy-going tolerance of sin. When presented to the Lord, our bodies belong utterly to him. Our own desires or preferences count for nothing. We belong entirely to him. So in looking for God's guidance we need constantly to remember that our bodies have been tied to the sacrificial altar as an offering for him for his service. We can no longer look selfishly for our own self-fulfilment, comfort or career prospects, but we humbly ask, 'Lord, what do you want me to do? And where do you want me to serve you? Anything, anywhere.' This, Paul says, is our 'spiritual worship'. We hear much these days about worship and its importance in the church. Romans 12:1 teaches us what is the fundamental nature of truly spiritual worship.

The offering of our bodies is here closely associated with a right use of our minds. How we think determines what we do. We cannot separate the sacrifice of our bodies from a renewed mind which will transform our whole life. No longer are we to be 'conformed to this world'. In an age when we are bombarded by the media, advertisements and fashion-consciousness it is not easy to discern how far the

Conditions for Guidance 243

world is influencing our thought patterns and therefore our attitudes and behaviour. But Paul exhorts us constantly to exercise biblical Christian thinking in all things.

We are being asked to abandon not only sinful habits of thought and action – they may be fairly easy to recognize if not to give up – but also attitudes which in themselves may seem harmless. It may never have occurred to us to question them. They are an ordinary fact of everyday living.

Now that we have seen a little more of what it means to prove or experience what God's will is, we must return to the main question of this book: How do we discover God's guidance? Perhaps the key to this question lies in Romans 12:1–2. We need first to soak ourselves in the biblical teaching concerning God's universal purposes of mercy, his will for the world and for his church. Only then should we be praying about our own part in the development of the whole history of God's relationship to his people. We will then ask the Lord how we personally fit into his overall purposes. What does he want to do for the world and the church, or for our own family, local situation or congregation? In this broader context the apostle Paul appeals to us to present our bodies as living sacrifices – and God himself will then surely direct us and instruct us according to his will.

Further Reading

G. Friesen, *Decision Making and the Will of God* (Multnomah Press, 1980).

E. V. Goldsmith, *Going places* (IVP/STL, 1979).

E. V. Goldsmith, *God can be trusted* (O.M., 1974).

M. C. Griffiths, *Don't Soft-pedal God's Call* (OMF, 1968).

M. C. Griffiths, *Give up your small ambitions* (IVP, 1970).

M. C. Griffiths, *Take my life* (IVP/STL, 1967).

T. Partridge, *Choosing your Vocation* (Marshalls, 1982).

M. Blaine Smith, *Knowing God's Will* (Ark Publishing, 1980).

G. Christian Weiss, *The Perfect Will of God* (Moody Press, 1950).

D. Willard, *In Search of Guidance* (Regal Books, 1984).

OMF, *When God Guides* (OMF, 1984).